ANOTHER DAY ON
WILLOW ST

a play

FRANK ANTHONY POLITO

WOODWARD AVENUE BOOKS
Detroit

FIRST EDITION
1 3 5 7 9 8 6 4 2

ISBN-13: 978-0-6923-4927-4
ISBN-10: 0-6923-4927-8

IMPORTANT BILLING & CREDIT REQUIREMENTS

The Licensee agrees that:

I. The Author shall receive billing as the sole author of the Play immediately beneath the title of the Play, on lines on which no other billing matter appears, as follows:

ANOTHER DAY ON WILLOW ST

a play by

Frank Anthony Polito

The name of the Author shall be at least 50% of the size of the title of the Play and shall be equal in size, type, coloring and/or boldness and shall appear in all programs, house-boards, billboards, displays, advertising, posters, circulars, throwaways, announcements and publicity for the Play, excepting only ABC ads in which only the title of the Play, theatre, and/or ticket prices are mentioned.

Only the name of the Licensee Producer and the title may precede the Author's name. No name except the title of the Play may be larger or more prominent in size, type, coloring and/or boldness than the Author's name.

II. Failure to comply with these stipulations will result in withdrawal of rights and in setting new terms consistent with Woodward Avenue Books company policy.

Praise for *Another Day on Willow St*

"Frank Anthony Polito's new play...owes a debt of gratitude to Thornton Wilder's *Our Town*, both being quiet plays about ordinary days and the remarkable moments within them. Yet *Another Day on Willow St* is very much its own rumination on relationships, communication, aspirations and disappointments. It touches the heart, elicits laughter and, by the final curtain, leaves us with something to think about."

— *DC Theatre Scene*

"An evocative new work that sends chills up your spine — it's an emotionally gripping drama that reminds audiences to cherish each and every day as no one can be certain what tomorrow brings... Playwright Frank Anthony Polito has managed to write a post-9/11 play that brings the tragedy of that historic event and the topic into focus in a subtle manner. One of the first of its kind where the focus is not on the tragedy itself or the aftermath... Polito's use of phrasing and scenic repetition is brilliant; creating a loop of life that is inescapable until it is not."

— *DC Metro Theater Arts*

"The relationship issues this fascinating and provocative new play delves into, the characters and their connections, the emotional and romantic resonances, are all unequivocally adult. Not in the naughty way. In the knotty way... *Another Day on Willow St* takes its sweet time introducing us to these two couples and their disparate yet parallel private lives... The languid exposition may leave one wondering, wherever is this going? But keep watching and listening — because where it's going gets deep."

— *Capital Gazette*

"Comprised of simultaneous settings in various cities, *Another Day on Willow St* is a series of conversations that take place two weeks before September 11, 2001. The conversations are brilliant in terms of the duet, trio, and quartet pairings that play off each other and intertwine as well. The entire production plays like a symphony."

— *MD Theatre Guide*

Another Day on Willow St was presented in February 2006 by the Carnegie Mellon School of Drama in Pittsburgh, PA. It was directed by Ed Iskandar. The cast was as follows:

IAN..Anthony Carrigan

PAUL...Rich Dreher

STACY..Liz Fenning

MARK..Paul Lindquist

Cast of *Another Day on Willow St*, produced by the Carnegie Mellon School of Drama, Pittsburgh, PA

(l. to r.) Paul Lindquist (Mark), Rich Dreher (Paul), Anthony Carrigan (Ian), and Liz Fenning (Stacy)

Photo: Frank Anthony Polito

Another Day on Willow St was presented in July 2007 as part of FutureFest at the Dayton Playhouse in Dayton, OH. It was directed by Fran Pesch. The cast was as follows:

IAN...Alex Carmichal

PAUL..Brian Buttrey

STACY...Lynn Kesson

MARK..Benjamin Norsworthy

Cast of *Another Day on Willow St*, produced by the
Dayton Playhouse, Dayton, OH

(l. to r.) Alex Carmichal (Ian), Lynn Kesson (Stacy),
Benjamin Norsworthy (Mark), Fran Pesch (Director),
and Brian Buttrey (Paul)

Photo: Dayton Playhouse

Another Day on Willow St was presented in August 2007 by Woodward Avenue Productions in association with Theater By The Blind at the New York International Fringe Festival. It was directed by Ike Schambelan. The cast was as follows:

IAN..Fred Backus

PAUL..Frank Anthony Polito

STACY...Pamela Sabaugh

MARK...Craig Bentley

Cast of *Another Day on Willow St*, produced by Woodward Avenue Productions in association with Theater By The Blind at the 2007 New York International Fringe Festival

(l. to r.) Craig Bentley (Mark), Frank Anthony Polito (Paul), Pamela Sabaugh (Stacy), and Fred Backus (Ian)

Photo: Andrew Fitch

Another Day on Willow St received its World Premiere in May 2014 at Compass Rose Theater in Annapolis, MD. It was directed by Lucinda Merry-Browne. The cast was as follows:

IAN..Ric Anderson

PAUL..Anthony Bosco

STACY..Renata Plecha

MARK..Jonathan Taylor

Cast of *Another Day on Willow St*, produced by
Compass Rose Theater, Annapolis, MD

(l. to r.) Ric Anderson (Ian), Renata Plecha (Stacy),
Lucinda Merry-Browne (Director), Jonathan Taylor (Mark),
and Anthony Bosco (Paul)

Photo: Stan Barouh

PLAYWRIGHT'S NOTE

In September 2001, I was living in Brooklyn. I worked as a publicist at a commercial book publisher in Manhattan, while also pursuing a career as an actor. I had only recently written my first play, *JOHN R*, which was being readied for a workshop by an off-off Broadway Theatre company in which my partner, Craig Bentley, and I were members.

Craig, also an actor, had just begun his graduate studies at the Academy for Classical Acting at the Shakespeare Theatre in Washington, DC — a one-year MFA program then in its second year. We were now living apart, confident that our long time relationship could survive the long distance.

Approximately 2 weeks after Craig had moved down to DC, I woke up late on a beautiful Tuesday morning, rushed past the volunteers reminding us to vote in the primary election that day, and rode the F train to my Midtown office. Arriving 20 minutes tardy, I snuck into the building, took the elevator up to the eerily quiet 8th floor where, surprisingly, no one was to be seen. After grabbing a cup of coffee in the kitchen (no time for Starbucks!), I sat down at my desk and began my morning routine of checking voice mails and emails.

Maybe 15 minutes later, the *ding!* of my Yahoo Messenger alerted me to a message from my brother back in Michigan, asking if I was okay.

And thus it all began...

Another Day on Willow St grew out of a one-act play I wrote during my first year of graduate studies at Carnegie Mellon called *Blue Tuesday*. The role of Ian Brown was played by a talented African-American actor, who later went on to a successful TV career (*Friday Night Lights*, *Grey's Anatomy*), named Gaius Charles.

I based the character on a man I'd read about who died in the World Trade Center on 9/11 — leaving behind his 8 months pregnant wife, the actress LaChanze, with whom I was familiar from the Broadway cast recording of the musical *Once on This Island*. I was delighted to have Gaius portray him.

When it came time to produce *Another Day on Willow St* as my thesis the following year, there unfortunately weren't any black actors available to play Ian Brown, so a white actor was cast. In 2007, for the workshop at the Fringe Festival in New York City that Craig and I were producing with our new Theatre company, Woodward Avenue Productions, my good friends Pamela Sabaugh and her (also white) husband, Fred Backus, portrayed the roles of Stacy and Ian. I felt that a real life couple would bring a special dynamic to the on-stage relationships; the same, albeit selfish, reason that Craig and I took on the roles of Mark and Paul.

For the World Premiere at Compass Rose, I left the casting to the Director of the wonderful production. Cindy also cast a white actor to play the role of Ian, and I was perfectly fine with her decision. An emerging playwright can't afford to be too demanding! And the success of the play isn't dependent on one character's race, I know perfectly well. But in my mind, Ian Brown would always be black.

Now, as I prepare the script for publication, I've made the conscious choice to list the character of Ian as being African-American. Not only do I feel that by having Stacy involved in an interracial marriage, it deepens her understanding of what Mark is faced with — dealing with his parents and their prejudices, along with society's — I'd also like to pay homage to the man on whom Ian Brown is based and to whom my play is dedicated.

Fred Anthony Polito

In memory of
Calvin J. Gooding

WHO

in order of appearance

IAN BROWN
an investment banker, age 40
African-American

PAUL GREEN
a lawyer, age 40

STACY GOLD
Ian's wife, age 40
Jewish

MARK GRAY
Paul's lover, age 40

WHERE

New York City, Boston & Provincetown

WHEN

Late summer, 2001

PROLOGUE

LIGHTS UP on IAN and PAUL both dressed for another day. THEY speak to the audience.

IAN. Tuesday morning...

PAUL. We lie in bed...

IAN. I stand by the bed...

PAUL. Breathing as one...

IAN. Watching her sleep...

PAUL. So peaceful.

IAN. So beautiful.

PAUL. Have a great day!

IAN. I love you.

PAUL. I love you.

IAN. Have a great day!

PAUL. Why does our time together never seem long enough?

IAN. Why does the call of duty always carry me away?

PAUL. It's just another day...

IAN. Like so many before it.

PAUL. Like so many before it...

IAN. It's just another day.

PAUL. Another day of airports...

IAN. Another day of office buildings.

PAUL. Of lovers living their lives apart...

IAN. Separated by distances long and short.

PAUL. It's the dawn of the New Millennium...

IAN. In the New York borough of Brooklyn...

PAUL. And this is just another day.

IAN. Another day on Willow Street.

LIGHTS FADE.

ACT I

SCENE 1

SOUND of telephone RING as STACY appears. SHE wears a headset, looking like a Time-Life operator, and sips a venti Starbucks iced coffee. SHE is very pregnant.

STACY. Jackie, hi! It's Stacy Gold at Random House calling, Tuesday August 28th, a little after 5 PM. I wanted to follow up on the galley I sent over... *What to Do When You Can't Find The One.* The author's flying in from Boston at the end of the week. I'm hoping you can squeeze her in for an interview...

SOUND of telephone RING as LIGHTS FADE on STACY, come UP on MARK, cell phone to his ear, sitting on a park bench.

MARK. Hey, Shep! It's Mark Gray, regarding the audition you sent me on last week. For the Macy's spot... It's like 5 o'clock on Tuesday. Just wanted to check in and see if you've heard anything back yet. The casting director was very complimentary...

SOUND of telephone RING as LIGHTS FADE on MARK, come UP on PAUL on his cell phone, sipping a Starbucks.

PAUL. Yes, this is Paul Green, calling for my mother's test results. The ones I brought her in for early last week... I believe you said you'd hear back from the lab no later than Tuesday at noon. It's now Tuesday after 5 and I'm starting to get concerned...

SOUND of telephone RING as LIGHTS FADE on PAUL, come UP on IAN on his cell phone.

IAN. Hey, Howard. Ian Brown. Sorry for the 5 o'clock fire drill on a Tuesday... What's the word up in Boston? We got this bake-off at the end of the week. My team's been busting their balls working on the pitch book. I tell ya, this IPO's gonna be bigger than Starbucks...

LIGHTS FADE on IAN, come UP on STACY.

STACY. Just a reminder, this is my last week in the office...

LIGHTS FADE on STACY, come UP on MARK.

MARK. Just to remind you, I'll be out of town for Labor Day...

LIGHTS FADE on MARK, come UP on PAUL.

PAUL. I'm heading out of town for the holiday...

LIGHTS FADE ON PAUL, come UP on IAN.

IAN. I know we got a holiday coming up...

LIGHTS FADE on IAN, come UP on STACY.

STACY. I'd love to speak
with you before I go.

*LIGHTS UP on
MARK.*

MARK. It would be great to
speak with you before I take
off.

*LIGHTS UP ON
PAUL.*

PAUL. You can reach me
on my cell phone any time.

*LIGHTS UP on
IAN.*

IAN. We can do the extra
face-time, no problem.

STACY. If you could give
me a call, that would be
awesome.

MARK. If you could call me
back, I'd appreciate it.

PAUL. Please get back to
me when you've got a mo-
ment.

IAN. Gimme a shout when
you get a sec, okay?

STACY. Bye-bye.

MARK. Bye now.

PAUL. Goodbye.

IAN. Later.

THEY hang up. LIGHTS FADE on MARK and PAUL.

STACY, still on her headset, makes another phone call.

STACY. Carol, hi! It's Stacy Gold at Random House...

IAN dials his cell phone. STACY's cell phone begins to RING. SHE checks the caller-ID display, continues with her pitch.

STACY. I wanted to follow up on the galley I sent over... *(STACY's cell continues to RING.)* What to Do When You Can't Find The One. *(STACY's cell continues to RING.)* If you could give me a call... *(SHE groans, clicks OFF her headset, answers her cell phone.)* Hello.

IAN. Hey, honey... It's me.

STACY. Hey, me.

IAN. Just wondering what my girls are up to...

STACY. Same thing we were up to half an hour ago when you called.

IAN. How's Oprah?

STACY. Her producer is being a total C-U Next Tuesday.

IAN. Honey... What did we say about subjecting our daughter to such language?

STACY. I've been pitching this stupid book to her for over two months. Either she wants it or she doesn't. But she needs to let me know — now. I've got plenty of other names in my Rolodex. *GMA, The Today Show...* Fox News Channel, for chris'sakes! Why's this bitch being such a total bitch? *(SHE covers her belly.)* Sorry...

IAN looks at STACY. THEY speak directly
to each other.

IAN. Remember what I told you? You don't gotta care anymore.

STACY. But I do.

IAN. It's not like they can fire you... Two more days, you're gonna walk out that door and "Bye-bye book publishing!"

STACY. In the meantime, I've got a million things on my plate.

IAN. Did you tell your authors you're leaving yet?

STACY. Make that a million and one.

IAN. You know what they say: "Procrastination is like masturbation... In the end, you're only screwing yourself."

STACY. Seriously... I should finish these calls before Steven totally freaks out.

IAN. I'll see you back in Brooklyn.

STACY. If you're still up.

IAN. Oh I'll be up.

STACY. Baby, please...

IAN. What?! *NYPD Blue* comes on at 10.

STACY. I can't remember the last time I turned on a TV, it wasn't to watch some shit-ass author hocking some shit-ass book on some shit-ass show I booked them on. *(SHE covers her belly.)* Sorry...

SOUND of telephone RING as LIGHTS
come UP on MARK, still sitting on his bench.

IAN. Hey, honey...

MARK checks the caller-ID on his cell phone, answers as PAUL appears.

STACY. Hey, what-y?

MARK. What's up?

IAN. I love you.

PAUL. I sure do miss you.

STACY. Love you too.

IAN and STACY hang up and FADE away.

MARK. I miss you too.

PAUL. What have you been doing since I left Brooklyn this morning?

MARK. Same thing I was doing when you called from the airport.

PAUL. How's the Promenade?

MARK. Totally packed from Pierrepont to Pineapple Street. I had to circle just to find a place to sit.

PAUL. Wish I was there to share your bench... How come these long weekends always seem so short?

MARK. We had three whole days together: Saturday, Sunday, and Monday.

PAUL. I would've tried for Tuesday if Mom didn't need me back in Boston.

MARK. How's she doing?

PAUL. Same pain, different day.

MARK. Did you talk to her doctor?

PAUL. Still waiting for a call back.

MARK. Welcome to my world.

PAUL. You haven't talked to your agent yet?

MARK. I had a lovely chat with his bitch. All of 22, he acts like he owns the agency. Meanwhile, I've been doing this since the brat was in diapers. I'm beginning to think he suspects I'm a homo...

PAUL. What makes you say that?

MARK. I'm ninety-nine percent positive he saw us at Stonewall after the Pride Parade.

PAUL. So...?

MARK. So... Everybody knows you can't make it in this business if you're —

> *HE stops himself.*

PAUL. A fag?

MARK. I hate that word.

> *PAUL looks at MARK. THEY speak directly to each other.*

PAUL. Remember what I told you? You shouldn't care so much.

MARK. But I do.

PAUL. It's not like Shep's going to drop you... In two more days, you'll get another audition and "Here we go again!"

MARK. In the meantime, I'll be at the gym.

PAUL. Say hi to Red Shirt.

MARK. I'll talk to you later, okay?

PAUL. The Michaels need to know if we're coming to P-town this weekend.

MARK. As long as I'm not shooting this commercial, we are.

PAUL. You know what a pill Michael P. can be...

MARK. Soon as I talk to Shep, I'll call you.

PAUL. Don't call me, call Shep... Make him start earning his ten percent.

MARK. You want me to piss him off? The guy barely sends me out as it is.

PAUL. All because his barely legal bitch thinks you're a flaming fag. *(beat)* Sorry...

MARK. Seriously... I should go before I change my mind about working out.

PAUL. Hey, hon...

MARK. Hey, what?

PAUL. I love you.

MARK. Love you too.

> *THEY hang up as LIGHTS FADE.*

SCENE 2

Wednesday. STACY enters her Willow Street brownstone, weighed down by the book bag slung over her shoulder.

STACY. Hello...?

SHE drops the bag on the table. After a moment, IAN appears from the other room.

IAN. Honey, you're home!

STACY. Sorry I'm late... Wednesday meeting with Steven went into overtime.

IAN kisses STACY, a short peck, then rubs her belly.

IAN. Hey there, Little Lahna. *(STACY lets out a gasp as the baby kicks.)* Whoa! Bet they felt that one back home in Jersey.

STACY. She's been like this all day.

IAN. Somebody's getting antsy.

STACY. Five more weeks.

IAN. Four weeks, five days.

STACY. Let's pray to God she lands on time... I'm telling you, I can't take it anymore. I'm the Goodyear blimp aloft over Manhattan in all its glory. *(SHE collapses on the sofa.)* Make that the Hindenburg, ready to come crashing down like a lead balloon.

IAN. You hungry?

STACY. Like this gut needs to become any more engorged.

IAN. But I made your favorite: Chicken Parm take-out from Café Buon Gusto.

STACY. It's a lucky thing you're cute.

IAN. I'm funny too.

STACY. I just need to lie here for a minute or two... Or twenty.

IAN. Somebody sure is lazy.

STACY. Somebody's been carrying around a basketball in her belly for thirty-five weeks.

> *IAN joins STACY on the sofa.*

IAN. I know what you need...

STACY. Baby, please... Why do you think I look like this?

> *IAN puts his arm around STACY, strokes her hair, rubs her belly.*

IAN. How was your day?

STACY. Another day at Random House. Got into the office around 7:30, waded through a few hundred emails. Marketing meeting, launch meeting, meeting with an editor. Phone call with a crazy author, phone call with a crazy author's crazy agent, phone call with an even crazier producer... And all before lunch.

IAN. I hope you stopped to eat something.

STACY. I sent Julienne to Starbucks. *(beat)* Of course she did nothing but bitch and complain about it. Evidently she missed the memo on being a good assistant. *And...* She totally got my drink wrong — again! How hard is it to remember, really? I order the same thing every time: iced decaf venti, sugar-free vanilla, nonfat, no whip, mocha.

IAN. Seems simple enough.

STACY. I swear if tomorrow wasn't my last day, I'd fire her 22-year-old ass already.

IAN. That's right! Come this time tomorrow, no more Julianne. No more crazy authors and crazy agents. And no more Random House.

STACY. You mean Juli*enne*.

IAN. That's what I said: Come this time tomorrow, no more Julienne. No more crazy authors and crazy agents. And no more Random House.

STACY. And not a moment too soon.

IAN. What are you gonna do with yourselves all day?

STACY. You're looking at it.

> *SOUND of telephone RING as MARK appears in his apartment, gym bag over his shoulder.*

IAN. Tell you what: how would you and Lahna like to do something special?

> *MARK checks the caller-ID as PAUL appears.*

MARK. What's up?

STACY. Some other time...

PAUL. Just walked in the door after another day of depositions...

STACY. Right now we're pooped.

MARK. And I just walked in the door after another day at the gym.

IAN. How's Sunday work
for you?

                    PAUL. How was it?

IAN. I got the whole day
free to spend alone with my
girls.

                    MARK. Same crowd, differ-
ent day.

     *STACY looks up at
IAN, barely awake.*

STACY. Brown Eyes.

                    PAUL. Was Red Shirt there?

IAN. That's me.

                    MARK. You sure are funny.

STACY. Take us to Coney
Island.

                    PAUL. I'm cute too.

IAN. "If that's what Mrs.
Brown wants..."

     LIGHTS FADE on IAN and STACY.

PAUL. What about Porn Star?

MARK. Surprisingly no Porn Star sighting today.

PAUL. He's probably off shooting a video someplace.

MARK. Probably... Someplace like Maui.

PAUL. I love Maui!

MARK. I know you do. *(beat)* Did you talk to your mom's
doctor yet?

PAUL. The man's got a degree from Columbia, he hasn't learned how to dial a phone.

MARK. Sounds like my agent — minus the degree from Columbia.

PAUL. Still no word from Macy's?

MARK. I wouldn't know... Still no word from Shep. And get this: now his bitch won't even take my call. What's he paying that kid for anyways?

PAUL. I can only imagine.

MARK. *(winces)* Ew.

> *PAUL looks at MARK. THEY speak directly*
> *to each other.*

PAUL. Aren't you getting tired of the whole actor-thing?

MARK. Are you getting tired of the whole lawyer-thing?

PAUL. Maybe you should pack up everything and move back to Boston.

MARK. And die a slow death! What the hell would I do in Boston?

PAUL. Same thing you're doing in Brooklyn... Only you'd be doing it here with me.

MARK. I can't do commercial work in Boston.

PAUL. You can do Theatre... At least in Boston you get paid to be in a play.

MARK. I got paid when I worked at the Present Company.

PAUL. Two hundred dollars for three weeks of rehearsal and a four week run. "It's not even minimum wage in Mexico."

MARK. See...? You loved that play! You're still quoting it.

PAUL. I loved *you* in that play... The lesbian sisters, I could do without.

MARK. At least the producers cared enough to compensate us.

PAUL. Too bad you can't make a living doing Theatre in New York... Unless you're a Broadway chorus boy.

MARK. Too bad I'm too old.

PAUL. Too bad you quit singing.

MARK. I never said I wanted to be on Broadway... All I need is one national commercial and I'm set.

PAUL So I've heard...

MARK I'm a good actor.

PAUL. You don't have to tell me... I'm your biggest fan.

MARK. Then why do you want me to give it all up?

PAUL. Seeing my mother like this is making me realize what's important: Love... Family... Commitment.

MARK. We got all those things.

PAUL. We don't got each other.

MARK. We will in three more days.

PAUL. Not if you're shooting some silly commercial. *(No response.)* Hello...?

MARK. I'm here.

PAUL. And I'm here.

> *THEY hold each other's gaze as LIGHTS FADE.*

SCENE 3

Thursday evening. STACY enters the brown-stone, gift bag in tow. SHE sets the bag on the table, holds her belly, begins to cry.

After a moment, IAN appears from the other room.

IAN. Happy Thursday!

STACY quickly dries her eyes.

STACY. Sorry I'm late... It took me forever to catch a cab.

IAN kisses STACY, a short peck, then rubs her belly.

IAN. Hey there, Little Lahna. *(HE holds STACY a moment.)* So how's it feel?

STACY. How does what feel?

IAN. Freedom.

STACY releases herself from IAN's embrace.

STACY. Absolutely awesome.

IAN. Where did they take you?

STACY. Serafina.

IAN. What did they get you?

STACY. You're looking at it.

IAN peeks into the gift bag, pulls out some baby toys.

IAN. That's all?! I hope you told 'em off like you said you were gonna.

STACY. I decided maybe it wasn't the best idea.

IAN. *Who* are you and *what* have you done with my wife?

STACY. I can't afford to go burning any bridges...

IAN. Burn away! You're never going back to that God forsaken place.

STACY. Steven said —

SHE stops herself.

IAN. What did Steven say? Hope he gave a big speech in your honor.

STACY. Steven had a dinner downtown.

IAN. Your own boss doesn't show up for your going away party? You're the goddamn Publicity Director! *(beat)* Sorry, Little Lahna.

STACY. *Former* Publicity Director.

IAN. Was Julianne there at least?

STACY. I don't know... Who's Julianne?

IAN. Julianne, your assistant.

STACY. *Former* assistant... Juli*enne.*

IAN. That's what I said: Your former assistant, Julienne.

STACY. Julienne went to the dinner with Steven... And she's no longer anyone's assistant. Steven promoted her at yesterday's meeting.

IAN. That girl moves fast! Bet she slept with the guy.

STACY. I highly doubt it.

IAN. I don't. At the Random House holiday party... She had two drinks, got all hands-y with me.

STACY. Steven is gay.

IAN. Steven your boss?

STACY. *Former* boss.

IAN. That's what I said: Steven your former boss is gay?

STACY. You've met the man, Ian... He sings show tunes in his office and does cartwheels down the hallway.

IAN. Well I hope you enjoyed your party... 'Cause you're outta there! Done. Finished. *Finito.*

STACY. The whole thing was fine... Till they all lined up, wanting to rub the Buddha. What is it about the bloated belly of the female human species that makes everyone and their brother think they're entitled to fondle it? It's like the core of my being has become this super-sized industrial strength magnet, growing more and more powerful with each passing day. I've become a planet from which no one can escape its gravitational pull. It's beyond their control. There's nothing they can do. They've just got to feel me up. I'm telling you, I can't take it anymore... The next time some random person asks permission to violate me, I swear to Holy God, I'm telling them to fuck off. *(SHE covers her belly.)* Sorry...

IAN. They're all just jealous of you.

STACY. Because I'm as big as a house?

IAN. 'Cause you're filled with life.

STACY. Well I'm sick and tired of being groped like some dirty whore.

> *SHE begins to cry.*

IAN. Honey... *(HE embraces her.)* What are you crying for?

STACY. Because I'm screwed... And not in a good way. What the hell was I thinking? Quitting my job! Now what am I going to do?

IAN. That's the beauty of it... You don't gotta do anything.

STACY. I've spent five days a week for the past fifteen years doing something... Now all of a sudden I'm supposed to do nothing?

IAN. I can't even remember the last time I had a day with nothing to do.

STACY. Then why didn't you quit your job instead of making me quit mine?

IAN. I didn't make — Is that what you think? 'Cause I thought the agreement was mutual.

STACY. I tried telling you I didn't want to.

IAN. When?

STACY. Right before I gave my notice.

IAN. What did I say?

STACY. "None of the other bankers' wives work."

IAN. So why should you?

STACY. Because... I need something to do.

IAN. Somebody's gotta take care of Lahna after she's born.

STACY. We could hire a nanny like everyone else.

IAN. And let some stranger raise our daughter?

STACY. It's not like I'd never be around.

IAN. The way my mother was around when I needed her?

STACY. Your mother didn't have a choice.

IAN. It's a free country...

STACY. Your mother had to work.

IAN. And you don't.

STACY. But I want to... Steven mentioned just yesterday, he still hasn't hired my replacement.

IAN. I thought he gave Julianne your job.

STACY. Juli*enne* isn't taking over as Publicity Director... She'd better not be! I can call Steven in the morning and see what he has to say.

IAN. In the morning, you're gonna sleep in. Then you're gonna go to Starbucks. Then you're gonna sit on the Promenade... And that's all you're gonna do.

STACY. Every day for the next four-and-a-half weeks?

IAN. This isn't part of The Plan.

STACY. Plans change.

IAN. Speaking of... I got some bad news about Sunday.

STACY. We're going to Coney Island on Sunday.

IAN. Not this Sunday... We got a client coming in from Boston.

STACY. So you've got to wine and dine him?

IAN. No... *We* gotta wine and dine him. He's bringing his wife.

STACY. Tell Howard you've already made plans.

IAN. Plans change.

STACY. Why are you so afraid of that man? You're the same age as he is.

IAN. Yeah but Howard's been CEO since he was like 30... I'm just a lowly underwriter.

STACY. He treats you like you're some kind of intern, not a Vice-President.

IAN. I may not be a Vice-President for much longer... Guess who's up for a promotion?

STACY. Congratulations.

IAN. I thought you'd be excited...

STACY. I am.

IAN. I'd hate to see you when you're pissed off.

STACY. I'm sorry, I just — What kind of person does business over Labor Day weekend?

IAN. One with a shit load of stock he's hired us to sell... *(beat)* Sorry, Little Lahna.

STACY. Which is why you keep kissing Howard's ass.

IAN. You met the guy, Stace... He eats babies for breakfast.

STACY. So much for Coney Island.

IAN. We can go some other time... Summer's not over yet.

STACY. It will be before we know it... Then fall, then winter, then what? A lot of days gone by and still no Coney Island.

IAN. That is not gonna happen.

STACY. It happens all the time. People put things off and put things off and put things off... Till one morning they wake up and find their life is over.

> *IAN places his hand on STACY's stomach.*

IAN. On the Buddha that is this belly, I swear: we will go to Coney Island... Just not on Sunday.

STACY. I suppose Rachel's going to be there.

IAN. He's Rachel's client too.

STACY. Better warn his wife.

IAN. Please don't, okay? This Boston deal is big time... My bonus could be almost double what it was last year.

STACY. What's the point in making all that money if you never have time to enjoy it?

IAN. I'll have plenty of time to enjoy it when I'm 50 and I retire.

STACY. What about right now?

IAN. Right now I'm hungry... Where's the take-out menus?

> *HE begins looking about the room. SOUND of telephone RING as MARK and PAUL appear, dimly lit, both on their cell phones.*

MARK. Go on...

STACY. I hear Monday's supposed to be nice...

PAUL. I can't...

IAN. Monday I work.

MARK Do it.

STACY. Monday is Labor Day.

PAUL. I'm embarrassed.

IAN. Have you ever seen Coney Island on a holiday?

MARK. *Now.*

STACY. I've never seen Coney Island period.

PAUL. I want you...

IAN. "If that's what Mrs. Brown wants..."

LIGHTS FADE on IAN and STACY.

MARK. You want me...?

PAUL. I want you...

MARK. You want me to what?

PAUL. I want you to go down on me.

MARK. You do?

PAUL. I do.

MARK. Yeah?

PAUL. Please.

MARK. Mmmmm...

PAUL. Mmmmm...

MARK. How's that feel?

PAUL. Nice.

MARK. You like that?

PAUL. Yeah...

MARK. That feel good?

PAUL. Yeah...

MARK. Mmmmm...

PAUL. Mmmmm...

MARK. Mmmmm...

PAUL. Mmmmm...

MARK. Mmmmm...

HE approaches orgasm.

PAUL. Wait a minute... Stop!

MARK. Out of all the gay lawyers in the world, I end up with Will from *Will & Grace*.

PAUL. That guy's not gay in real life, you know?

MARK. I'm beginning to think neither are you... You're such a prude.

PAUL. I'm not a prude. I'm a total fag. *(beat)* Sorry...

MARK. When was the last time you showered at the gym?

PAUL. I go to the gym to work out... Not to flirt.

MARK. After five years, it was bound to happen... You don't find me attractive anymore.

PAUL. Have you walked past a mirror lately? You're hot.

> *MARK looks at PAUL. THEY speak directly to each other.*

MARK. Do you still love me?

PAUL. I tell you I love you all the time.

MARK. I can't remember what you feel like...

PAUL. I'll make it up to you this weekend in P-town, I promise.

MARK. When we first started dating, you couldn't get enough. The bedroom, the bathroom, the living room floor...

PAUL. Don't remind me... That hideous Ikea rug.

MARK. Remember the time in my kitchen?

PAUL. Which one?

MARK. Exactly!

PAUL. My aching back remembers the table top.

MARK. You loved it.

PAUL. I did.

MARK. But not anymore?

PAUL. Not over the phone.

MARK. When you're horny and you live in separate states...

PAUL. So give up that tiny apartment and move in here with me. Rent free! The condo's practically paid for...

MARK. I'm a 40-year-old man with a Master's degree...

PAUL. In Shakespeare.

MARK. I can take care of myself.

PAUL. What about in ten years when you're 50?

MARK. Even if I did come back to Boston, we could never live together the way we did in Manhattan.

PAUL. We could if you told your parents about me.

MARK. They know about you...

PAUL. They know I'm your friend... Not your lover.

MARK. I hate that word.

PAUL. But it's true.

MARK. I'm perfectly well aware.

PAUL. So are your parents.

MARK. Then why do I have to tell them at all?

PAUL. You're a 40-year-old *gay* man with a lover of five years... Draw a diagram.

MARK. I told you how it had to be when we started dating.

PAUL. Don't you want to celebrate the holidays together for once in our lives?

MARK. Believe me... You do not wanna have Christmas dinner with Barkeep Bob and Helen the Happy Home-maker.

PAUL. Other married couples have to suffer... Why should we get off so easily?

MARK. We're not a married couple.

PAUL. But we could be.

MARK. We will be... Someday.

PAUL. You act like you're ashamed of us.

MARK. I'm not ashamed — Is that what you think? 'Cause I thought everybody who counts already knows we're a couple.

PAUL. Everybody except for your parents.

MARK. If I tell them about us, everything's going to change.

PAUL. That's kind of the point...

MARK. You know how my mom gets... She was Ellen DeGeneres' biggest fan. Till she came out. Now every time she sees her it's "Ellen the Dyke!"

PAUL. How are you going to feel if *your* mother dies and you still haven't said a word?

MARK. At least she'll go to her grave loving me.

PAUL. Do you even love her?

MARK. She's my mother... What kinda question is that?

PAUL. One I'd like for you to answer.

MARK. Of course I love her.

PAUL. Since I've known you, I've never once heard you tell her... You tell your father all the time.

MARK. That's 'cause he says it first.

PAUL. So start with him.

MARK. I can't.

PAUL. My parents know about me.

MARK. Your parents aren't Catholic.

PAUL. They're Jewish.

MARK. It's not the same thing.

PAUL. Might as well be.

MARK. Your parents are divorced... You hardly ever see your dad.

PAUL. Which makes it even worse I'm about to lose my mom... I spoke to her doctor — *finally!* He's giving her three to five months.

MARK. No...

PAUL. Which is why I need you to do something.

MARK. Anything.

PAUL. Before she dies... My mother wants us to get married.

MARK. You said you wouldn't marry me.

PAUL. I said I wouldn't marry you unless you invite your parents to the wedding.

MARK. But to do that, I'd have to tell them I'm —

    HE stops himself.

PAUL. Now's your big chance... Unless you don't want to marry me.

MARK. You know I do.

PAUL. Then what are we waiting for?

> *THEY hold each other's gaze as LIGHTS FADE.*

SCENE 4

Friday morning. STACY appears in the brown-stone, a sweater around her shoulders. SHE looks about the empty room then holds her belly. After a moment, SHE spies a note on the table.

STACY. *(reading)* "Enjoy your first day of freedom... I love you... Ian."

SHE picks up the TV remote and points. SOUND of Today Show. SHE flips through the channels. SOUND of Regis & Kelly. SHE flips through again. SOUND of Jerry Springer. SHE stares at the TV, mesmerized.

SOUND of telephone RING as MARK appears in his apartment, gym bag over his shoulder, talking on his cell.

MARK. Hey, Shep! *(Pause.)* It's Mark Gray. *(Pause.)* I'm good, thanks... What's up? *(Pause.)* You're kidding? I got it! *(Pause.)* No... No plans the whole weekend. *(Pause.)* Uh-huh... Uh-huh... You too. *(HE hangs up.)* Now what?

MARK gathers his things and heads out. STACY snaps herself out of her reverie. SHE clicks off the TV, finds her cell, dials.

STACY. Good morning, Julienne! *(Pause.)* It's Stacy. *(Pause.)* Fine, thanks... How's everything up there? *(Pause.)* You're kidding? You booked *Oprah*! *(Pause.)* No... No plans all day. *(Pause.)* Uh-huh... Uh-huh... You too. *(SHE hangs up.)* Now what?

STACY gathers her things and heads out as MARK arrives on the Promenade. HE finds an empty bench, takes a seat.

After a moment, MARK pulls out his cell phone and dials. SOUND of telephone RING as PAUL appears, sipping a Starbucks.

PAUL. Hey, hon.

MARK. What's up?

PAUL. Just now getting into the office... The line at Starbucks was out the door and around the corner.

MARK. You should've tried the one across the street.

PAUL. The barista never gets my name right... What sane person would call their kid Ball? B-A-L-L. Clearly I said *Paul.* P-A-U-L. As in Paul Newman. Paul McCartney —

MARK. Paul Lynde?

PAUL. I was going to say The Apostle.

MARK. Same difference.

PAUL. Sorry, I'm a little over-caffeinated this morning... Mom woke me up at 6, ringing my cell phone.

MARK. Is everything okay?

PAUL. She wants us to stop by before we take off tonight... What time's your train get in?

MARK. Actually, I got some bad news... Good news for me but bad news for us. Shep called. I booked the job.

PAUL. Congratulations.

MARK. I thought you'd be excited.

PAUL. I am.

MARK. It's a lucky thing you're not the actor.

PAUL. I'm sorry, I just — *(HE looks at MARK. THEY speak directly to each other.)* What kind of commercial shoots over Labor Day weekend?

MARK. One that's paying me a shit load of money.

PAUL. So much for P-town.

MARK. We can go some other time... Summer's not over yet.

PAUL. What'll I tell the Michaels?

MARK. Tell them I have to work.

PAUL. But Michael W. rented a house for four.

MARK. It's Labor Day weekend in P-town... You can find another gay guy to go with you.

PAUL. What about your Uncle Gene?

MARK. Uncle Gene's already got a place in P-town.

PAUL. This could be your last chance to see him.

MARK. And they say I'm the drama queen.

PAUL. The man's not getting any younger... Or healthier.

MARK. He's *my* Uncle Gene... Quit your worrying, okay?

PAUL. I can't live like this anymore.

MARK. We'll see each other again next weekend.

PAUL. I'm not talking about the long distance.

> *HE hangs up and FADES away as STACY arrives on the Promenade, Starbucks in hand. SHE looks around for an empty bench, finds none.*
>
> *After a moment, STACY takes out her cell phone and dials. SOUND of telephone RING as IAN appears on his cell.*

IAN. Hey, honey.

STACY. It's me.

IAN. Hey, me.

STACY. How's your day?

> *IAN's attention is diverted, OFF.*

IAN. *(shouts)* One sec, Rachel! I'll be right in... *(to STACY)* Another day on Wall Street.

STACY. I won't keep you.

IAN. Oh yes, you will... So what are my girls up to this morning?

STACY. Taking a walk on the Promenade across the river... Can you see us?

IAN. Lemme take a peek... *(HE looks at STACY. THEY speak directly to each other.)* There you are!

STACY. It sure is a gorgeous day.

IAN. Too bad I'm stuck all the way up here... How's our little Buddha?

STACY. Being a royal pain in my side... 4 o'clock this morning, I wake up to her playing kickball with my kidneys.

IAN. I woke up early too.

STACY. What's your excuse?

IAN. I kept thinking about Lahna... How our life's gonna be after she's born... All the things we're gonna do together... What she's gonna look like.

STACY. I hope she has your eyes.

IAN. You do?

STACY. That way, whenever you're not around, I can look at her and see you staring back.

IAN. You sure are sweet.

STACY. Not as sweet as you.

Again IAN's attention is diverted, OFF.

IAN *(shouts)* Rachel! I got a cell phone up to my head... Gimme a sec, okay? *(to STACY)* I should probably get over to the conference room. We got a meeting with Howard in five...

STACY. What time will you be out of there tonight?

IAN. With any luck, I should walk out the door by 6:30... 7 at the latest. *(shouts, OFF)* Jesus Christ, Rachel! Quit busting my balls, would ya? *(to STACY)* Honey, I'll see you back in Brooklyn.

HE hangs up his cell phone and FADES away.

STACY. I love you. *(No response.)* Hello...?

On his bench, MARK pulls out a copy of Back Stage. HE notices STACY standing nearby.

MARK. Excuse me?

STACY turns to MARK.

STACY. He didn't say "I love you."

MARK. I'm sorry. *(beat)* Would you like to sit?

STACY takes a seat beside MARK on the bench. SHE sips her coffee in silence as MARK flips thorough his paper.

STACY. Who knew it would be so crowded down here on a Friday morning?

MARK. Yeah it's pretty much Baby Central this time of day... All the moms and nannies out with their big-wheeled strollers.

STACY. I don't think I'll ever get over this view.

MARK. Why live in Manhattan when you can sit and look at it from over here?

STACY. Amen! I had a place in Midtown for almost a decade... You know how much money I could've spent on shoes if it weren't for my rent?

MARK. About as much money as I could've spent on shoes if it weren't for *my* rent.

STACY. You like shoes?

MARK. Is *Harry Potter* the greatest book ever written?

STACY. You like *Harry Potter?*

MARK. I love *Harry Potter!*

STACY. Oh my god... I've read them all. *Prisoner of Azkaban* is by far my fave.

MARK. Do not say a word! I'm still buried deep within the *Sorcerer's Stone*.

STACY. Someone's got some catching up to do.

MARK. I can't even believe I'm reading a children's book.

STACY. *Harry Potter* is not a children's book.

MARK. Tell that to Barnes & Noble... I found my copy in the Children's section, right between *Sweet Valley High* and *The Giving Tree*.

STACY. Trust me, I work in book publishing... *Harry Potter* is a #1 National Bestseller. Over 200 million copies sold to date.

MARK. What I wouldn't give to be J.K. *(pronounces it like "howling")* Rowling right about now.

STACY. *(pronounces it like "bowling")* J.K. Row-ling.

MARK. That's what I said: What I wouldn't give to be J.K. *Rowling* right about now.

STACY. The movie comes out November 16th... Better get reading!

MARK. *(gestures to his paper)* Believe me, I'd much rather waste my time with *Harry Potter* than this depressing piece of crap.

STACY. *Back Stage?* I had a feeling you're an actor...

MARK. What gave me away? The desperation in my voice.

STACY. There's just something about you. A confidence. Like you know exactly who you are, and you're not afraid to admit it. To anyone.

MARK. That's me... Mr. Confidence.

STACY. What kind of acting do you do? Maybe I've seen your work.

MARK. I doubt it... My claim to fame is serving salad to Meryl Streep on film.

STACY. I love Meryl Streep! What movie?

MARK. *One True Thing.*

STACY. You're right, I missed it.

MARK. You and everybody else. I was pretty much a glorified extra...

STACY. Still... You got to work with Meryl Streep. How many actors can say that?

MARK. Robert DeNiro... Kevin Kline... Cher.

STACY. Stop!

MARK. I did get my own trailer... And Meryl Streep even spoke to me, off camera.

STACY. Please tell me she was nice.

MARK. So nice!

STACY. What did she say?

MARK. Between takes, William Hurt asks me where I'm from. I say: "New York." He says: "No... Where are you from, really?" So I say: "Boston." To which Meryl Streep replies: "I love Boston!" Then on the next take, I knock over her water glass with my tongs, the director yells: *"Cut!"* Like he's totally pissed 'cause I ruined the shot. Meryl Streep looks up at me, smiles, and says: "Thank you! I was acting terribly."

STACY. Oh my god... Love her! *(beat)* You've got a great voice, by the way. Not a hint of desperation. I bet you sing beautifully.

MARK. I did... Back in college, I used to take lessons from this amazing opera diva. She'd sit at the piano wearing this fancy fox fur draped delicately over her shoulders. And she'd coo — in French — at her infant daughter asleep in her bassinet by her side.

STACY. How sweet!

MARK. How depressing! That baby is now a senior at Boston College. Whatever... I've turned my back on the Theatre.

STACY. But I love the Theatre!

MARK. Too bad you can't make a living at it... Unless you're a Broadway chorus boy. Which I will never be.

STACY. It's a shame you stopped singing... My brother Jeffrey's partner is a big Broadway producer.

STACY. He could totally get you an audition for one of his big Broadway musicals.

MARK. Musicals, plural?! That's okay... I'm a total sell-out. Right now I'm focusing on commercials.

STACY. And how's that working out for you?

MARK. Actually, pretty decent... I just booked a job this morning.

STACY. *Mazel tov!*

MARK. To be honest, I think I got it 'cause I fit the suit.

STACY. You got it because you're a talented actor. And before you say: "How would *you* know?" I'll tell you... I have a sixth sense. Whenever I meet someone, not a thing gets past me. Try as you might, there's no hiding *who* you are or *what* you do. Like the first day I'm introduced to my boss, Steven, I could totally tell he's gay. Even before he came out to anyone in the office — and he's worked there for like forever. Of course he belted out the theme to *Maude* a minute after we met... But that's not what gave him away.

MARK. Don't tell me... Your sixth sense?

STACY. Exactly! So what's the commercial?

MARK. Um... It's a holiday spot. For Macy's.

STACY. Somehow I don't peg you as the Santa-type. What are you? His Little Helper.

MARK. It's like I got the word *ELF* tattooed in the middle of my middle-aged forehead.

STACY. Since when is 29 middle-aged?

MARK. So much for your sixth sense... Say hello to 40.

STACY. Not so fast, bub... I don't climb over that hill till next week Tuesday.

MARK. Happy Birthday!

STACY. Does this *punim* look happy? So tell me more about Macy's... I bet you're super cute in your little elf hat and your little elf tights.

MARK. 'Cause candy cane stripes are the ultimate in *haute couture*.

STACY. Your parents must be proud.

MARK. *(changing the subject)* What is it *you* do for a living?

STACY. You're looking at it.

    SHE takes a sip of her Starbucks.

MARK. Wait — I thought you were in book publishing.

STACY. Not anymore. As of today, this working girl is officially retired.

MARK. And you're not even 40... Must be nice!

STACY. Get back to me a month from now.

    SHE sips her Starbucks.

MARK. I still haven't quite gotten the whole Starbucks-thing, myself. My buddy Paul... Total Starbucks junkie. We can't go anywhere near a Starbucks, he doesn't gotta have a chai latte. Me, I'm like: "Why should I pay three dollars for burnt-tasting coffee?"

STACY. Chai is tea.

MARK. And why is small *tall* and medium *grand*?

STACY. Grande.

MARK. It tastes burnt.

STACY. Well I love it. *(SHE takes a big sip.)* Back in my twenties, I was this hard-core workaholic. I'm talking balls-to-the-wall, ten hours a day if it wasn't twelve. Fuel up on coffee, lock myself in my office, make my assistant answer all my calls. Never go out to lunch unless it's business-related. Work, work, work. Go home. Sleep. Wake up, do it all over again.

MARK. But did you enjoy it?

STACY. I'm beginning to realize just how much.

MARK. So why did you give it up?

STACY. It's all part of The Plan.

MARK. The Plan?

STACY. Get married, get pregnant, quit my job, have a baby.

MARK. Whose plan is that?

STACY. My husband Ian's. *(SHE lets out a gasp as the baby kicks.)* I know, I know... *(SHE rubs her belly.)* She hates it when I badmouth her daddy.

MARK. You're having a girl?

STACY. I'd better be... Otherwise, my son's going to be wearing a ton of pink.

MARK. Have you chosen a name for her yet?

STACY. Lahna.

MARK. That's a pretty name...

STACY. With an *H. (beat)* Ian picked it out. *(SHE lets out a gasp as the baby kicks again.)* I know, I know...

MARK. L-A-N-A-H?

STACY. L-A-*H*-N-A.

MARK. Why not plain old L-A-N-A? It worked for Lana Turner. Landed her seven different husbands and eight different weddings.

STACY. I know, right? Unfortunately, L-A-N-A spelled backward is...

MARK. Gotcha.

STACY. You know how cruel kids can be.

MARK. Say no more... "Been there *and* got the T-shirt." *(HE waves at STACY's belly.)* Hey there, Little Lahna... *(to STACY)* Would you mind if I...?

> *STACY hesitates a moment.*

STACY. Fuck off.

MARK. I'm sorry... I didn't mean to —

STACY. No, no! That was just something I had to get out. Please...

> *STACY places MARK's hand on her belly. SHE lets out a gasp as the baby kicks.*

MARK. Did you feel that?

STACY. She must really like you.

MARK. You think?

STACY. She doesn't do that for everyone.

> *STACY begins audibly sipping her iced coffee.*

MARK. I don't think you're gonna get any more out of that.

STACY. Sorry...

> *SHE sips the last drop.*

MARK. Was that one of those fancy Frappuccino-things?

STACY. This was an iced decaf venti, sugar-free vanilla, nonfat, no whip, mocha.

MARK. How the hell do you remember all that?

STACY. Say it three times a day for five years straight.

MARK. I can't imagine what it must be like.

STACY. You're obviously not a junkie.

MARK. I mean creating another life with the person you love... Somebody who's a part of you both.

STACY. You won't know till you give it a try.

MARK. I'd like to... Someday.

STACY. Then what are you waiting for?

MARK. I'm — *(HE stops himself.)* Not married.

STACY. And that's got *what* to do with the price of chai at Starbucks?

MARK. I guess I just never saw myself standing at the front of a church, waiting for some woman in white to come marching down the aisle.

STACY. Can I tell *you* a secret? Something I haven't told anyone... Not even my husband.

MARK. What are total strangers for?

STACY. I'm terrified to have this baby... Every time I think about it, my head starts spinning, my heart starts racing...

MARK. Try cutting back on the caffeine.

STACY. I can barely breathe.

MARK. I know exactly how you feel. The whole idea of giving up everything for another person... Doesn't get much scarier than that.

STACY. So I'm not totally crazy?

MARK. You are! But so am I.

STACY. My name's Stacy, by the way...

MARK. Hey, Stacy. I'm Mark.

> *LIGHTS FADE on the Promenade, come UP on the brownstone as IAN enters. HE carries a plastic bag of freshly pressed shirts.*

IAN. Honey...? *(HE hangs up the shirts.)* Stacy...?

> *STACY appears. SHE looks groggy.*

STACY. What time is it?

IAN. 7:40.

STACY. We were beginning to think you were never coming home... We fell asleep waiting.

IAN. Can't say I blame you...

> *HE collapses on the sofa, closes his eyes.*

STACY. Was there a problem with the train?

IAN. Same old 2/3 we know and hate.

STACY. Your office is only a few stops away.

IAN. I dropped by the cleaners.

STACY. The one up on Montague?

IAN. No the one up in Harlem... Where else would I go?

STACY. You forgot something...

IAN. I'm sorry... You should've called me.

> *STACY sits beside IAN. SHE kisses him.*

STACY. Baby, you look exhausted.

IAN. After twelve hours, I'm surprised I look that good. *(HE rubs STACY's belly.)* Hey there, Little Lahna.

STACY. What time did you go in this morning?

IAN. 7... Wait — what day is today? Friday... Today I went in at 6.

> *STACY pats her stomach.*

STACY. Someone's getting hungry.

IAN. Like daughter, like mother.

STACY. You're not ready for dinner?

IAN. Honey, I just walked in the door.

STACY. There's a new little place down on Smith Street... I thought we could check it out.

IAN. What's wrong with Joya?

STACY. Nothing's wrong with Joya... I love Joya! Maybe we should try something new.

IAN. When we already know what we like and where to find it at?

STACY. Aren't you getting bored with the same thing all the time?

IAN. Not when it tastes so good.

> *HE kisses STACY, a short peck.*

STACY. It's a lucky thing you're cute.

IAN. I'm funny too.

STACY. Fine... We'll go to Joya.

IAN. Do I detect a tone?

STACY. There's no tone.

IAN. Ah! There it is again.

STACY. It's nothing...

IAN. Which means *something*.

STACY. Summer's almost over... Makes me sad just thinking about it.

IAN. Don't be sad. We're gonna have our own little baby before we know it... Then you'll never be sad again.

> *STACY touches IAN's face.*

STACY. Brown Eyes.

IAN. That's me.

STACY. Ready?

IAN. Ready.

> *HE does not move.*

STACY. Just let me grab my sweater and we can go.

> *SHE pulls herself away, exits. After a moment, IAN calls out.*

IAN. How was your big first day off?

STACY *(off)* It was fine.

IAN. What did you end up doing with yourselves?

STACY *(off)* We slept in... Then we went to Starbucks... Then we sat on the Promenade.

> *STACY returns, sweater in hand, to find IAN still on the sofa.*

STACY. Just like you said we should. *(beat)* Someone sure is lazy.

IAN. Five more minutes.

STACY. You know how crowded Joya gets.

IAN. You're no fun anymore.

STACY. After almost five years, what do you expect?

> *IAN rises from the sofa.*

IAN. What happened to the girl I met that night at Rudy's?

STACY. You knocked her up and now she's a heifer.

IAN. Bet she can still cut a rug.

> *HE embraces STACY, twirls her about.*

STACY. Stop!

IAN. Make me. *(HE dances with her a moment.)* I gotta say, that Rudy's had one helluva jukebox.

STACY. It's a lucky thing I asked you to dance.

IAN. It's a lucky thing I lived right around the corner.

STACY. So it was all about the bar and not the girl?

IAN. And that Johnny... Now he could pour a pint.

STACY. If that's how you feel, why didn't you marry Johnny?

IAN. I didn't fall in love with Johnny.

STACY. Why not? He sure was cute.

IAN. Why didn't *you* marry Johnny?

STACY. He didn't have your eyes.

IAN. What am I gonna do with you?

STACY. Take us to dinner.

IAN. But they're playing our song.

STACY. Billie Holiday can wait. Your daughter's appetite won't.

    IAN talks to STACY's belly.

IAN. Lahna... Tell Mommy she shouldn't blame everything on you.

STACY. Tell Daddy he shouldn't procrastinate so much... It's like masturbation. *(beat)* We did meet this guy...

IAN. Oh really... Where, what's his name, what's he do?

STACY. On the Promenade. Mark. He's an actor.

IAN. I bet he is!

STACY. He invited us to share his bench.

IAN. I bet he did! I see how this works... You get a day off, you spend it with some other guy.

STACY. Only because we couldn't spend it with you. *(SHE kisses IAN.)* Shall we?

IAN. You wanna walk or you wanna take a cab? It's a beautiful night...

STACY. Why don't we take the car?

IAN. There's never anywhere to park.

STACY. What's the point in owning a Prius if we hardly ever drive it?

IAN. We drive it.

STACY. When?

IAN. To see my family.

STACY. Jersey doesn't count.

IAN. To see your family.

STACY. We always take the train to Connecticut.

IAN. Tell you what: we can drive the car out to Coney Island on Monday... Unless you wanna take the subway.

STACY. We'll take a cab.

> *SHE exits the brownstone. IAN follows as LIGHTS FADE.*

SCENE 5

Sunday evening. PAUL sits alone at a bar in Provincetown. After a moment, HE takes out his cell phone, dials.

LIGHTS UP on MARK as his cell begins to RING. HE checks the caller-ID, answers.

MARK. What's up?

PAUL. Hey, lover.

MARK. How's P-town?

PAUL. "Men, men, everywhere!"

MARK. "And not a drop to drink?"

PAUL. *Au contraire, mon père!* You should see the sides of beef runnin' around this joint.

MARK. On a Sunday?

PAUL. Woof!

MARK. I'll ignore that... Only 'cause you're drunk-y.

PAUL. I'm not drunk-y. *(HE downs his cocktail.)* Now I'm drunk-y.

MARK. Where are you?

PAUL. The Little Bar... You're missin' out on all the Labor Day Eve excitement.

MARK. Are the Michaels behaving themselves?

PAUL. Those old queens! They're back at the house watchin' *Golden Girls* reruns on Lifetime.

MARK. Well that sucks... I hate thinking of you in P-town all alone-ly.

PAUL. I'm not alone-ly, hon...

MARK. Who are you out getting drunk-y with?

PAUL. Tim's here... Somewhere.

> *MARK looks at PAUL. THEY speak directly to each other.*

MARK. Who's Tim?

PAUL. Tim... From dart league.

MARK. I can't keep track of all your new Boston friends.

PAUL. I told you 'bout Tim... Months ago. He's a Jew... Went to Harvard... Total top.

MARK. That makes *two* things you got in common.

PAUL. You know what the say: "Opposites attract."

MARK. Does Tim know the Michaels?

PAUL. He knows them now... He's stayin' at the house.

MARK. Oh really... I'm surprised Michael P. let you invite a stranger... He hates new people.

PAUL. Not when they look like Tim.

MARK. So what have you guys been doing all weekend?

PAUL. Oh the usual... Goin' out to dinner... Goin' dancin'.

MARK. The Michaels don't go dancing.

PAUL. Who said anything about the Michaels?

MARK. What else have you and *Tim* been up to?

PAUL. Mostly we just hang out an' talk.

MARK. We talk all the time.

PAUL. But you're not here.

MARK. Does Tim have a boyfriend?

PAUL. Not that I'm aware of...

MARK. Is he looking for one?

PAUL. I doubt it... He's recently divorced. *(beat)* From a woman.

MARK. So this Tim guy's pretty hot?

PAUL. If you're into former straight guys an' BMWs.

MARK. Obviously you are...

PAUL. And you aren't?

MARK. You drive a Mercedes.

PAUL. What's Red Shirt drive?

MARK. I don't give a flying fuck about Red Shirt! Did you sleep with Tim?

PAUL. Tim is just a friend.

MARK. Do you wanna sleep with him?

PAUL. It's not about sex.

MARK. What's it about then?

PAUL. Havin' someone who's around.

MARK. If you want Tim, all you gotta do is tell me.

PAUL. I want *you.*

MARK. Then why did you bring him up?

PAUL. I hurt.

MARK. I'm sorry... Don't cry.

PAUL. I'm not.

> *HE wipes his tears.*

MARK. Do you want what happened to my Uncle Gene to happen to me?

PAUL. Your mother won't stop talkin' to you if she finds out you're gay.

MARK. She hasn't said a word to him since the day he told her... As far as she's concerned "Homo Gene" is already dead.

PAUL. And pretty soon, so will my mother be.

MARK. Please don't, okay?

PAUL. Jesus Christ! The woman is *dying*... She wants one tiny little thing before she leaves this shit hole world — an' you won't give it to her.

MARK. I'm sorry.

PAUL. Stop sayin' that! If you were truly sorry, you'd get off your ass and do somethin' about it.

MARK. There's nothing I can do, okay?

PAUL. I will not be the guy standin' at your funeral everyone thinks is just your friend.

MARK. You won't be.

PAUL. Why should I believe you?

MARK. 'Cause I said so.

PAUL. It's not enough anymore.

> LIGHTS UP on STACY as SHE bursts into
> the brownstone followed by IAN.

IAN. Honey...?

               MARK. I'm their only son...

IAN. Stacy...?

> MARK. You know what it's gonna do to my folks if they find out I'm a fag?

IAN. Okay, I get it... You're pissed off.

> PAUL. You know what it's going to do to *us* if they don't?

LIGHTS FADE on MARK and PAUL.

IAN. Wanna tell me why?

STACY. First I'm dragged to a dinner I don't even want to be at... Then I'm forced to entertain your client's Townie wife the entire evening... On top of the fact, I get stuck sitting next to Rachel.

IAN. You sure are pretty when you're jealous.

STACY. I'm not jealous.

IAN. What did Rachel ever do to you?

STACY. Nothing. She's just so... *Rachel.* With her perfect smile and her perfect hair and her perfect —

SHE stops herself.

IAN. Tits?

STACY. She wasn't born with those.

IAN. I don't care.

STACY. Of course you don't... You're a man.

IAN. I don't care 'cause I'm not interested.

STACY. Why not? She's gorgeous.

IAN. You know what they say: "Takes one to know one."

STACY. I'm a cow.

IAN. But you're my cow.

STACY. You're just saying that because I'm the mother of your child.

IAN. Damn straight! And you're all the more beautiful 'cause of it.

STACY. You lied to me... Two days ago you stood here and said we could drive the car out to Coney Island on Monday. Now you pull this shit! Were you even planning on telling me? Or was I going to wake up tomorrow morning and discover one of your love notes: "Sorry about Coney Island, honey... Have a nice day."

IAN. Howard just sprung it on me... Right before the risotto.

STACY. You don't even like to play golf!

IAN. Tell that to Howard.

STACY. Why can't Rachel take the guy? He's her client too.

IAN. Yeah right... I can just see Rachel on the golf course in her five-inch fuck-me pumps.

STACY. If she wasn't a dirty whore...

IAN. I'm not saying she's not a whore... But come on already!

STACY. What about Howard? He's the boss.

IAN. Which is why he's got other plans.

STACY. And you don't?

IAN. He's the goddamn CEO of the company... You want me to tell Howard Lutnick he can't spend Labor Day with his wife and kids?

STACY. 11 months... Almost an entire year. You've been promising to take me to Coney Island since the day we moved to Brooklyn.

IAN. We will go to Coney Island... I promise.

STACY. That's what you keep saying! And yet the second something else comes up, you totally change your tune... STACY. Especially if it's got anything to do with fucking Cantor Fitzgerald.

IAN. You know the plan, Stace... Ten more years and then I'm free.

STACY. Ten more years will be too late.

IAN. Is one of us going somewhere?

STACY. We don't have much time left.

IAN. We got our whole lives.

STACY. Four weeks and one day... Then no more quiet dinners just Ian and Stacy. No more lying in bed together just Ian and Stacy. No more *anything* just Ian and Stacy... Ever again.

IAN. If that's how you feel... Why are we having this baby?

> *LIGHTS FADE.*

<u>END OF ACT I</u>

ACT II

SCENE 1

Labor Day. MARK sits on the Promenade sipping a Starbucks coffee. After a moment, HE dials his cell phone.

MARK. Hey, Paul. It's me... Happy Labor Day! Too bad you're not here. I'm sitting on the Promenade in your favorite spot...

STACY appears, Starbucks in hand. SHE looks about for an empty bench, sees MARK.

MARK. Sorry about last night... Give me a buzz when you get this, okay?

HE hangs up his cell as STACY approaches.

STACY. Fancy meeting you here... How was Macy's?

MARK. Have you ever noticed the word Santa is an anagram of *Satan*?

STACY. My parents sure did... Good old Murray and Sylvia Gold! Growing up in Greenwich, my brother Jeffrey and I begged for a Christmas tree. We never got so much as a Hanukkah bush. *(beat)* You want some company?

MARK. They say misery loves it, don't they?

STACY. They also say it helps if you talk about it.

MARK. Who are *they* anyways — and what gives them all the answers?

STACY takes a seat on the bench. THEY sit in silence a moment.

STACY. I don't think I'll ever get over this view.

MARK. Why live in Manhattan when you can sit and look at it from over here?

HE sips his coffee.

STACY. Well something must be afoot.

MARK. 'Cause I look like hell?

STACY. Because you're drinking Starbucks!

MARK. I gotta admit: it doesn't taste nearly as burnt as I remembered.

STACY. Rough night?

MARK. I'll spare you the boring details.

STACY. What are total strangers for?

MARK. My buddy Paul... We got in this argument... To say I didn't get much sleep would be an understatement.

STACY. Friends argue...

MARK. That's the thing... We never used to.

STACY. You'll work it out... Just give it some time.

MARK. Only there's not much left. Paul's mom... Her whole life, she's a total goody-two-shoes. "Don't drink, don't smoke..." What does she do? Goes to the doctor one day... Stage four ovarian cancer. Paul's been taking care of her the past six months —

STACY's cell phone RINGS.

STACY. Remember the days you'd leave your apartment knowing you might just miss a call... But it was a chance you were willing to take? *(SHE checks the caller-ID, groans.)* It's Ian... Give me a minute to get rid of him. *(SHE answers her cell as IAN appears.)* Yes?

IAN. Hey, honey... It's me. *(No response.)* Just wondering what my girls are up to this morning.

STACY. We're sitting on the Promenade drinking our Starbucks. *(beat)* With Mark.

IAN. Who's Mark?

STACY. Shows how you listen.

IAN. Bench guy?

STACY. How's golf?

IAN. Don't ask.

STACY. So it's not a total waste of time?

IAN. Looks like we're gonna be a while.

> STACY *looks at* IAN. THEY *speak directly to each other.*

STACY. Could you define a while?

IAN. Howard called...

STACY. That'll teach you to pick up the phone.

IAN. Like I had a choice.

STACY. It's a free country...

IAN. He wants me to take Boston IPO out for dinner and drinks.

STACY. On Labor Day... Take him out where?

IAN. Um... He said something about Scores.

STACY. Of course he did.

IAN. I hate that place.

STACY. Because ogling a bunch of naked women is such a chore.

IAN's attention is diverted, OFF.

IAN. *(shouts)* Lookin' good, buddy! *(to STACY)* They're not naked.

STACY. Might as well be.

IAN. Remember rule one of investment banking? "Without the clients, we're nothing."

STACY. What if I need you?

IAN. I'll keep my cell phone on vibrate. *(No response.)* Four weeks. 28 days. I promise... Nothing is gonna happen before then.

STACY. How can you be so sure?

IAN. Tell you what: you and Lahna go out to dinner... Wherever you want. My treat.

STACY. In case you haven't noticed, our daughter's not much of a conversationalist.

IAN. So invite one of your friends along... Call up Julianne. See how she's doing.

STACY. Her name is Juli*enne*... And she isn't my friend. And in case you've forgotten, today is a holiday.

IAN. For chris'sakes, would you stop acting like it's Thanksgiving or Christmas? It's goddamn Labor Day!

STACY. All my friends are having dinner with their husbands... Who are *home.*

IAN. I'm sorry... Don't cry.

STACY. I'm not.

SHE wipes her tears.

IAN. I gotta go, it's my putt... I'll call you from the cab later.

STACY. What time will that be?

Again, IAN's attention is diverted, OFF.

IAN. Dude! Check you out... You da man!

STACY. Hello?

IAN. I'm here.

STACY. And I'm here.

SHE hangs up and IAN FADES away.

STACY. I can't live like this anymore.

MARK. Bad news?

STACY. Just typical Ian... His boss is *making* him have dinner with a client.

MARK. So what are you ladies doing for grub?

STACY. Good question... Lahna's a big Lean Cuisine fan.

MARK. I make a mean spinach quiche, if I do say so myself.

STACY. Lahna loves spinach quiche!

MARK. Maybe she'd care to join me.

STACY. I'm thinking she might need a chaperone.

MARK. Hmmmm... Wonder where we could get one on such short notice?

STACY. Perhaps I could be persuaded.

MARK. I invited Ben & Jerry.

STACY. In that case... Just tell us when and where.

MARK. 7 o'clock. 128 Willow Street... Between Pierrepont and Clark.

STACY. Get out! We live at *126* Willow Street... Between Pierrepont and Clark.

MARK. You get out!

STACY. The brownstone with the —

MARK. Oh I'm familiar... Must be nice!

STACY. You know what they say: "You've seen one..."

MARK. That's not what I say... I say: "How the hell can you afford the rent?"

STACY. We own it, actually.

MARK. Must be nice!

STACY. My husband works on Wall Street.

MARK. Which explains how you live on Willow Street.

STACY. *You* live on Willow Street.

MARK. In a space the size of your stoop!

STACY. I'm surprised we haven't seen each other around...

MARK. That's New York City for ya! The only place you can practically live on top of somebody and never even know it.

> *THEY clink Starbucks cups.*

STACY. So tell me more about Paul...

> *LIGHTS FADE on STACY and MARK, come UP on PAUL in MARK's apartment. HE positions himself seductively somewhere.*
>
> *After a moment, MARK appears, toting a brown paper grocery bag.*

PAUL. Hey, lover...

MARK. What happened to P-Town?

PAUL. It wasn't any fun without you.

MARK. What happened to Tim?

PAUL. He wasn't you.

HE kisses MARK deeply.

MARK. You never kiss me like that.

PAUL. That's because you don't like my kisses.

MARK. I love your kisses.

THEY kiss again.

PAUL. What's in the bag, fag? *(beat)* Sorry...

MARK. You sure are funny.

PAUL. I'm cute too.

MARK. I ran up to Key Food... I got a friend coming over.

PAUL. What's his name?

MARK. A *female* friend.

PAUL. Remind me to take away your gay card.

MARK. She's my neighbor... I'm making her dinner.

PAUL. No you're not... You've got other plans.

MARK. But the quiche is already in the oven.

PAUL. You're making quiche? Oh hon...

MARK. I thought you liked my quiche.

PAUL. I like your kielbasa even better.

HE goes for MARK's zipper.

MARK. Don't!

PAUL. But I've been looking forward to seeing you all day.

MARK. You're seeing me right now.

PAUL. I mean *all* of you.

> *HE tries peeling off MARK's shirt.*

MARK. Would you please stop?

PAUL. Well this is a first.

MARK. I know! Look at you... One weekend apart, suddenly you're Chester the Molester.

PAUL. You know what they say: "Use it or lose it."

MARK. Believe me... I use it a lot.

PAUL. With Red Shirt, maybe.

MARK. Be nice...

PAUL. I'd rather be naughty.

MARK. *Who* are you and *what* have you done with my boyfriend?

PAUL. I don't like it when we argue.

MARK. Neither do I.

PAUL. Let me show you how sorry I am.

> *HE begins kissing MARK's neck.*

MARK. I feel bad.

PAUL. But you taste good.

MARK. She's all alone... She's pregnant.

PAUL. An unwed mother? Mark, really...

MARK. She's married.

PAUL. So where's her husband?

MARK. Off at some tittie bar with some client.

PAUL. I love it when you talk butch.

MARK. I'm butch.

PAUL. Hon... You've got a quiche in the oven and your girlfriend coming over for a pajama party.

MARK. She's not my girlfriend... And she's not spending the night.

PAUL. Damn straight! I am.

MARK. She's Jewish...

PAUL. So that means we'll automatically get along? Like Shmoyna Pipik and Hester Herbonowitz Rosenblatt, sitting around *kibitzing* in their *shmatas*.

MARK. Who's Shmoyna Pipik and Hester Herbono...?

PAUL. Ditch the chick.

MARK. You can't just burst in here out of the blue and start ordering me around.

PAUL. Oh I'll order you around.

MARK. What's gotten into you?

PAUL. Nothing... Yet.

> *MARK hesitates then dials his cell phone.*

MARK. Stacy, hi. It's Mark... Sorry, I gotta cancel dinner. My buddy Paul's in town from Boston, totally unexpected... Give me a buzz when you get this, okay?

> *HE hangs up.*

PAUL. Don't you mean *fuck* buddy?

MARK. What did I say?

PAUL. You're doing it again.

MARK. I'm not doing anything.

PAUL. She doesn't know you're gay, does she?

MARK. I haven't exactly told her, if that's what you mean.

PAUL. Why am I not surprised?

MARK. I never got a chance.

> *PAUL goes into lawyer mode.*

PAUL. How long have you known this Stacy person?

MARK. Not long...

PAUL. Does she talk to you about her husband?

MARK. A little...

PAUL. But you know she has one at least?

MARK. I do.

PAUL. And *how* do you know this? Because she told you!

MARK. I was just telling Stacy about you this afternoon.

PAUL. Oh really... And did you tell her I'm your lover?

MARK. I hate that word.

PAUL. Lover, lover, lover!

MARK. I like her.

PAUL. And she obviously won't like you back if she finds out you pack fudge in your free time.

MARK. You have no idea how it is... You weren't even gay till you met me.

PAUL. Don't flatter yourself.

MARK. So I wasn't your first boyfriend ever?

PAUL. You were... I took one look at that big — *smile* of yours, I had to jump right on it.

MARK. Guys like you think coming out is so easy.

PAUL. You mean boyishly cute, charming lawyer-types?

MARK. I mean the ones who do it at 35 after realizing they really don't wanna have sex with girls... The ones who were popular in high school and never grew up being called queer or sissy or Mark *Gay*.

PAUL. I'm beginning to think you're homophobic.

MARK. I'm not homophobic.

PAUL. Then why won't you hold my hand whenever we walk down Christopher Street?

MARK. It's uncomfortable... I never know whose hand goes on top.

PAUL. Jesus Christ! It's the year 2001... Why do you still give a fuck what people think?

MARK. Maybe I don't wanna be a stereotype.

> *SOUND of doorbell BUZZ.*

PAUL. Guess Fertile Myrtle needs to learn how to check her voice mail.

MARK. Would you please not be an asshole?

PAUL. "Hello, Pot... This is Kettle... You're black."

MARK. I'll tell her.

> *HE buzzes STACY in.*

PAUL. After you tell your parents?

MARK. Stop being such a dick.

PAUL. Stop lying to your friend.

MARK. I didn't lie...

PAUL. You didn't exactly tell her the truth.

MARK. It's not like it's the first thing that comes out of my mouth when I meet somebody: "I'm Mark Gray... I like cock."

> *STACY appears.*

STACY. Hey, new best friend...

MARK. Stacy, hey... Didn't you get my message?

> *STACY checks her cell phone.*

STACY. Oh look... One missed call: Mark Gay. *(beat)* Oops! Forgot the R.

PAUL. You must be Stacy...

STACY. Sorry, I didn't realize you had company.

PAUL. I'm Paul Green... Mark's *buddy* from Boston.

STACY. So you're Paul! Mark's told me all about you...

PAUL. Did he tell you I'm his — ?

MARK. Best friend! You bet I did.

PAUL. Anything else?

MARK. You know, the basics: You're Jewish... You went to Harvard... You're a class action —

PAUL. Mark, don't be rude... Stacy, you were saying?

STACY. Um... You're Jewish. You went to Harvard. You're a class action lawyer...

MARK. The *best* class action lawyer.

STACY. And you're a total Starbucks junkie.

PAUL. So all the important stuff.

MARK. 'Fraid I'm fresh out of Starbucks, you two... Stacy, can I offer you anything else?

STACY. A glass of water would be awesome... Of course I'll probably pee it all out the minute I consume it. I swear I've got the bladder of a Chihuahua. Before I got pregnant, I could totally go for *hours* without making a trip to the ladies' room. Sometimes the entire day... I'd be sitting at my desk, writing some press release or pitching some producer at some show somewhere... All of a sudden I'm like: "Why am I crossing my legs like a virgin at a frat party?"

MARK. Is sparkling okay?

PAUL. So much for not wanting to be a stereotype.

STACY. Good old New York City tap is terrific.

MARK. Make yourself at home... The bathroom is down the hall if you need it. First door on the left.

PAUL. The only door on the left. *(to STACY)* This place is such a closet.

> *MARK shoots PAUL a look as HE exits to the kitchen. STACY takes in the apartment.*

STACY. I love these curtains! Are they Pottery Barn?

PAUL. They're Martha Stewart.

STACY. I love Martha Stewart!

PAUL. So does Mark.

STACY. What a great space... It's so warm and cozy.

PAUL. If by warm and cozy you mean *small.*

STACY. Please! You should've seen my studio in Manhattan... Talk about living in a closet.

MARK returns with a glass of water.

MARK. Here you go... New York's finest. What did I miss?

PAUL. Stacy... Did Mark tell you about the apartment we shared in Chelsea? It was the cutest one bedroom.

STACY. I love Chelsea! Whereabouts?

MARK. 22nd Street.

PAUL. Right above the gay bar.

MARK. Between 7th and 8th.

STACY. Barracuda!

MARK. Closer to 8th.

PAUL. You know it?

STACY. I used to go there with my brother Jeffrey all the time... "Back in the day."

PAUL. *(to MARK)* I didn't realize Stacy had a gay brother.

MARK. And a gay boss... His name's Steven.

STACY. *Former* boss.

PAUL. *(to STACY)* What does Jeffrey do for a living? If I might be so bold as to inquire.

MARK. Enquiring minds! Always wanna know...

STACY. He's an orthopedic surgeon at Beth Israel.

PAUL. A gay Jewish doctor? *Shalom!*

MARK. Paul...

PAUL. He isn't single, by any chance? I know the perfect guy...

MARK. Paul...

STACY. I'm afraid he isn't. In fact, Jeffrey and his partner Daniel just got married in Maui.

PAUL. *Mazel tov!*

MARK. Paul loves Maui.

STACY. Talk about a gorgeous event... Luau, pig roast, the whole "Book 'em Danno!" Made mine and Ian's wedding come off like a country hoe down.

PAUL. I'm sure Jeffrey and Daniel looked amazing together.

STACY. Like two Hebrew gods in matching Versace tuxes! And when they slipped into their Speedos after the ceremony...

PAUL. *Oy vey!* Got any pictures?

MARK. So your brother's a doctor, Stacy! Your parents must be proud.

STACY. Oh my god... He's like their wet dream come true.

PAUL. Despite the fact that he's a *faygeleh*?

MARK. Paul!

STACY. He's their only son... All Murray and Sylvia want is for Jeffrey to be happy.

PAUL. Of course... What parent wouldn't? *(HE shoots a look at MARK then back to STACY.)* So what does Daniel do?

STACY. He's a Broadway producer.

MARK. A *big* Broadway producer.

STACY. Musicals, mostly.

PAUL. Mark loves muscles — I mean *musicals*.

STACY. I bet Daniel could get you tickets to his latest show, Mark... If you're interested.

MARK. Sure... What's the show?

STACY. Well it's off-Broadway, actually. At the Actors Playhouse... *Naked Boys Singing*.

MARK. I wouldn't say I love muscles — I mean *musicals*.

PAUL. Yes you do... Tell Stacy your favorite musical of all time.

MARK. Do I have one?

PAUL. Does Liza spell Liza with a Z? Wait till you get a load of this, Stacy. Go on, Mark... Spill.

MARK. I guess it would have to be... Either *Oklahoma!* or *Hello, Dolly!* Anything with an exclamation point.

PAUL. He is such a liar... As long as I've known him, it's always been *Xanadu*.

STACY. I love *Xanadu*!

MARK. *Xanadu* is a movie.

PAUL. It's still a musical.

STACY. I remember I used to have the soundtrack...

PAUL. With the purple and the pink — ? So did Mark!

STACY. I knew all the words to every song.

PAUL. So did Mark!

STACY. I used to put on my Walkman and roller skate around pretending I was Olivia Newton-John.

PAUL. So did —

MARK. Smells like the quiche is burning!

STACY. Oh my god... We should get Daniel to produce a Broadway musical of *Xanadu.*

MARK. You can't put *Xanadu* on stage... It would never work.

PAUL. It's too bad Mark gave up singing, Stacy. Maybe Daniel could help him land a part...

STACY. That's what I said.

PAUL. If he played his casting couch right.

MARK. The quiche!

PAUL. Maybe you should go check on it... I'll stay here with Stacy.

STACY. Go ahead, Mark... Paul and I can entertain ourselves.

MARK. Don't *kibitz* about anything too exciting without me.

> *HE exits into the kitchen.*

STACY. That Mark sure is a great guy.

PAUL. He has his moments.

STACY. How long have you been... Best friends?

PAUL. Five years this past June 23rd.

STACY. I bet he makes a good one.

PAUL. Most of the time.

STACY. He really cares about you.

PAUL. Sometimes I wonder.

STACY. You'd be a fool not to notice. *(beat)* So how did you two meet?

PAUL. You don't want to hear all the boring details...

STACY. Would I ask if I didn't?

PAUL. Let's see… 1996. I get dragged to this God awful play at this God awful theatre. One of those East Village holes in the wall. Guess who's the star of the show? Good old Mark Gray from South Boston… A few years prior, I'd seen him in this fantastic production up at Merrimack Rep. I remember being so impressed with the guy's performance, I thought about sticking around after and asking for an autograph…

STACY. Mark's first fan!

PAUL. More like his first stalker… Too bad I couldn't bring myself to do it.

STACY. Why not? Mark would've totally been flattered.

PAUL. Back then, I wasn't — *(HE stops himself.)* I was *shy*… But this time, no way was I missing out.

> *MARK returns, unseen by PAUL.*

PAUL. So there I am, waiting at the stage door — program in hand — ready for him to sign it. Talk about *shpilkes*! Finally he comes out and I'm like: "Excuse me, Mr. Gray…" And he's like —

> *MARK looks at PAUL. THEY speak directly to each other.*

MARK. "Do I know you?"

PAUL. "Not yet… But you will."

STACY. Five years? That's a long time.

PAUL. Tell me about it… Five years being best friends with this guy.

MARK. I'm sorry, Stacy…

STACY. For what?

MARK. Paul's not my buddy... He's my lover.

PAUL. He hates that word.

MARK. But it's true.

STACY. I had a feeling that might be the case.

MARK. I suppose I'm pretty obvious.

STACY. I wouldn't say you're *obvious*. But come on... How many 40-year-old never-been-married straight actors do you know in New York City?

MARK Will you forgive me?

STACY. To be honest, I'm a little offended.

MARK. I never meant to lie to you.

STACY. Did you really think I'd mind?

PAUL. Mark has this ridiculous fear people won't like him if they find out he's a Friend of Olivia.

STACY. That is totally ridiculous... How could anyone not like Mark?

PAUL. That's what I keep telling him... Maybe he'll finally listen to you.

STACY. If anything, you should be proud. You make a beautiful couple... So when's the big day?

MARK. Soon as I have The Talk with my parents.

STACY. Mark...

MARK. I know.

STACY. How long have you been together?

PAUL. Don't look at me.

STACY. Have your parents ever met Paul?

MARK. Once, twice...

PAUL. "Three times a lady."

STACY. And did they know you lived together? In Chelsea!

MARK. They did.

PAUL. Not that they ever came to visit.

STACY. And you think they still don't know you're a couple?

MARK. I've been meaning to tell them... I just haven't found the right time.

STACY. Sweetie, there's no such thing. Do yourself a favor... Stop putting it off. You owe it to yourself... And to Paul.

PAUL. I just knew we were going to get along! *(HE extends a hand to STACY.)* Shmoyna Pipik? Hester Herbonowitz Rosenblatt.

MARK. Who's Shmoyna Pipik and Hester Herbono...?!

PAUL. Forget it! You're not a Jew... You wouldn't understand.

STACY. *(to MARK)* So... You'll have The Talk with your parents?

MARK. I will.

PAUL. When?

MARK. Soon.

PAUL. Promise?

　　　　LIGHTS FADE.

INTERLUDE

LIGHTS UP on IAN and PAUL both dressed for another day. THEY speak to the audience.

IAN. Tuesday morning...

PAUL. We lie in bed...

IAN. I stand by the bed...

PAUL. Breathing as one...

IAN. Watching her sleep...

PAUL. So peaceful.

IAN. So beautiful.

PAUL. Have a great day!

IAN. I love you.

PAUL. I love you.

IAN. Have a great day!

PAUL. Why does our time together never seem long enough?

IAN. Why does the call of duty always carry me away?

PAUL. It's just another day...

IAN. Like so many before it.

PAUL. Like so many before it...

IAN. It's just another day.

PAUL. Another day of airports...

IAN. Another day of office buildings.

PAUL. Of lovers living their lives apart...

IAN. Separated by distances long and short.

PAUL. It's a beautiful morning in the borough of Brooklyn...

IAN. A beautiful morning in historic Brooklyn Heights...

PAUL. And this is just another day.

IAN. Another day on Willow Street.

PAUL. Outside the weather is perfect...

IAN. A perfect day outside...

PAUL. Not a cloud in the sky...

IAN. The sky so blue...

PAUL. It's the most beautiful day I've ever seen.

IAN. The most beautiful day.

LIGHTS FADE.

SCENE 2

SOUND of telephone RING as MARK appears, cell phone to his ear.

MARK. What's up?

PAUL appears on his cell phone.

PAUL. Guess who I ran into on my way home from the office? I was grabbing a slice at Pinocchio's...

MARK. Matt Damon?

PAUL. Even better... Your father.

MARK. Did you say hello?

PAUL. You bet I did.

MARK. What was my dad doing in Cambridge?

PAUL. Hell if I know... I was too busy drooling.

MARK. *(winces)* Ew.

PAUL. I can't help it the man's hot.

MARK. He's 60 years old!

PAUL. If I wasn't already dating his son...

MARK. Okay... Now you're grossing me out.

PAUL. He invited me to drop by next time you're in town.

MARK. See...? My dad likes you.

PAUL. Guess Barkeep Bob took the news better than you thought he would.

MARK. Actually, I haven't talked to him yet.

PAUL looks at MARK. THEY speak directly to each other.

PAUL. What have you been doing since I left Brooklyn this morning?

MARK. Um... Stuff.

PAUL. No wonder he was so nice... Boy do I feel like a dumbass!

MARK. It's been twenty-four hours...

PAUL. It'll be a week before you know it... Then a month, then a year, then what? A lot of days gone by and still no ring on my finger.

MARK. That is not gonna happen.

PAUL. It happens all the time. People put things off and put things off and put things off... Till one morning they wake up and find their life is over.

MARK. I swear to you, I will talk to my folks... Just not today.

PAUL. You stood in your apartment last night and you promised... Right in front of Stacy.

> *STACY appears in the brownstone. SHE rubs her belly, singing softly.*

STACY. "Another day..."

> MARK. For chris'sakes, they're my parents.

STACY. "Another day on Willow Street..."

> PAUL. And I'm your *lover.*

> *LIGHTS FADE on MARK and PAUL as IAN enters the brownstone.*

IAN. Hey, honey.

STACY. "Another day on Wall Street?"

IAN. I'm sorry.

STACY. For what?

IAN. Coming home late.

STACY. Anything else?

IAN. I'm sorry I couldn't answer when you called.

STACY. You want to know what amazes me about you, Ian? You screw up and you don't even realize it.

IAN. I got stuck in a meeting...

STACY. We had a reservation... An hour ago... At the River Café.

IAN. Oh shit.

STACY. Oh shit is right.

IAN. Today's Tuesday?

STACY. All day.

IAN. I kept thinking it was Monday.

STACY. That's because yesterday was a holiday and you spent it golfing.

IAN. Why didn't you remind me this morning when we talked?

STACY. I shouldn't have to remind you it's my *birthday*.

IAN. You know what they say: "The way for a man to remember his wife's birthday is to forget it once." *(No response.)* It's not like I forgot on purpose... Work was crazy today.

STACY. As opposed to every other day?

IAN. One of my clients called... His analyst completely blew it. He threatened to go to another bank.

STACY. So let Howard handle it... He's the goddamn CEO of the company.

IAN. Howard was at a meeting, out of the office, with Rachel.

STACY. Where — Motel 6?

IAN. I'll ignore that... Only 'cause of what day it is today.

STACY. Remember what a big deal turning 40 was for you? I threw you that huge surprise party with all your friends.

IAN. You never said you wanted a party.

STACY. We were supposed to spend tonight together... Just the two of us.

IAN. And I'm here now... Let's go out.

STACY. It's too late.

IAN. It's barely 9 o'clock.

STACY. I'm not talking about the time.

IAN. What about all the nights you came home late from Random House? And HarperCollins... I never said a word or got pissed off at you.

STACY. Don't you dare put this on me! You're the one with the lousy memory. Oh and by the way... Our anniversary's coming up. A week from today.

IAN. I know when our anniversary is... September —

> *HE stops himself.*

STACY. 11th.

IAN's cell phone RINGS. HE checks the caller-ID, groans.

STACY. You're not going to get that.

IAN answers his cell.

IAN. Hey, Howard... *(Pause.)* Tomorrow morning at La-Guardia? Tell Rachel I'll meet her at the gate... *(Pause.)* You got it! Later. *(HE hangs up.)* Need any baked beans? I got a 7 AM shuttle to Boston.

STACY. Weren't you with that guy all weekend?

IAN. Now we gotta meet with the board. Shouldn't take more than a day... Two tops. I'll be back by Friday.

STACY. We've got child birthing class on Thursday night.

IAN. Funny, this is the first I'm hearing of it.

STACY. 8 o'clock... I signed us up weeks ago, remember?

IAN. I wouldn't forget something important like child birthing class.

STACY. You forgot my birthday.

IAN. I didn't forget, I just —

STACY. Forgot?

IAN. You're right, Stace, I'm a horrible human being... Why don't you just go without me?

STACY. It's the first class... I can't be the only woman there without her husband.

IAN. You should've thought of that when you signed us up and forgot to tell me.

STACY. I told you!

IAN. When?

STACY. I don't know...

IAN. That's what I thought.

> *LIGHTS FADE.*

SCENE 3

Wednesday, early evening. MARK appears in his apartment, cell phone in hand. After a moment, HE dials.

MARK. *(slipping into a Southie accent)* Hey, Pop. It's ya son... Ya got a minute? *(Pause.)* What's up? *(Pause.)* No... When's the fun'ral? *(Pause.)* Tell Ma I'll take the train up on Friday. *(Pause.)* Nothin'... It can wait. *(Pause.)* Love ya too.

LIGHTS FADE on MARK as STACY appears on the Promenade.

STACY. See that itty-bitty lady way out there with her arm held up high... Isn't she pretty, Lahna? Someday when you're a big girl, Daddy and I will take you to meet her. We'll go on a big boat, and we'll climb up to the top of her crown, and we'll see all of New York City. Won't that be fun? We'll do lots of fun things with your daddy... Once he doesn't have to work so hard anymore.

LIGHTS FADE on STACY, come UP on IAN and PAUL sitting together at a bar over empty drinks.

PAUL. As much as I'd like to... Today's only Wednesday.

IAN. What's-a matter — you a light-weight or somethin'?

PAUL. Ya know what they say: "Friends don't let friends drive drunk."

IAN. It's a lucky thing we're strangers.

PAUL. I should prob'ly take off.

IAN. An' leave me here all by my lonesome? I thought Boston's the City of Brotherly Love.

PAUL. Philadelphia. *(beat)* I suppose it *could* be Boston. Dependin' on the bar you're in. Unfortunately, Top o' the Hub ain't the spot.

IAN. C'mon! Ya got a wife an' kids waitin' at home or somethin'?

PAUL. No... But I got a *lover* expectin' me to call.

IAN. So give the guy a ring... I can wait.

LIGHTS UP on STACY as MARK appears on the Promenade.

PAUL. So can he.

LIGHTS FADE on IAN and PAUL.

MARK. There she is... The Belle of Brooklyn Heights!

STACY. I don't think I'll ever get over this view.

MARK. Why live in Manhattan when you can sit and look at it from over here?

HE presents STACY with a Starbucks coffee.

STACY. Is that...?

MARK. Iced decaf venti, sugar-free vanilla, nonfat, no whip, mocha.

STACY. You, my friend, would make the perfect assistant.

SHE takes a big sip.

MARK. Rough night?

STACY. I'll spare you the boring details.

MARK. What did Mr. Wall Street do this time?

STACY. Oh nothing... Yesterday was only my birthday — and Ian totally forgot.

LIGHTS UP on IAN and PAUL at the bar.

IAN. Uh-oh... Somebody's
in the dog house.

MARK. He'll make it up to
you, I'm sure.

PAUL. I'm sure your wife's
wonderin' where you're at...

STACY. He left this morning
on a business trip... With *Rachel.*

IAN. You talkin' 'bout Rachel?

MARK. You're not a fan, I
take it.

PAUL. I take it she isn't
your wife.

STACY. Hell no! She's a dirty
whore.

IAN. Hell no! She's a
whore.

STACY. Sometimes I wonder
why I ever married that man.

IAN. I'm married to some-
body else...

STACY. I was perfectly fine
dating fool after fool and feeling nothing...

IAN. A wonderful woman
I feel nothin' but love an'
respect for.

STACY. Then in he walks one night and ruins it all.

IAN. Why'd I have to go an' ruin it all?

MARK. In he walks where?

PAUL. So where'd ya meet her?

STACY. Rudy's.

IAN. Ever been to Rudy's?

MARK. The dive bar with the giant pig out front?

PAUL. The pig bar on 9th Avenue?

STACY. I practically lived there when I first moved to Midtown.

IAN. Cheap beer, best jukebox in all-a Midtown.

STACY. All the free hot dogs a girl can ask for.

IAN. Don't forget the free hot dogs.

STACY. I'd stop by on my way home, sit at the bar.

IAN. I'd sit at the bar, do my own thing.

MARK. You went to the pig bar alone?

PAUL. You hung out at
Rudy's alone?

> STACY. I'm a JAP from
> Connecticut... I can take care
> of myself.

IAN. I grew up in New-
ark... I can handle myself.

> STACY. Why can't I just sit
> there and mind my own busi-
> ness?

IAN. There I am, mindin'
my own business...

> STACY. Me and Johnny
> Walker.

IAN. Me and Jimmy Beam.

> STACY. Why do I insist on
> looking over at him — sitting
> all alone in the corner —
> looking so sad with those
> beautiful brown eyes?

*STACY looks at IAN. THEY speak directly
to each other.*

STACY. Hey, I'm Stacy... Wanna dance?

IAN. Hey, Stacy. I'm Ian... You bet.

LIGHTS FADE on IAN and PAUL.

MARK. So how long have you and Ian been married anyways?

STACY. Five years, next week Tuesday.

MARK. Happy Anniversary!

STACY. I'll be lucky if Ian remembers...

MARK. What kinda man forgets his own anniversary?

STACY. Same man who forgets his wife's birthday.

> *LIGHTS FADE on MARK and STACY,*
> *come UP on IAN and PAUL still at the bar.*

IAN. I'm havin' a baby... My wife, I mean. She's havin' a baby... I mean it's my baby too... *Our* baby.

PAUL. Congratulations.

IAN. 36 and 2/7 weeks.

PAUL. So what's that in real time?

IAN. 254 days.

PAUL. What kinda man knows that?

IAN. One who's been waitin' 254 days to be a father.

PAUL. Then what're ya doin' leavin' her home by herself?

IAN. Now ya sound just like her. Ev'rything I'm doin', it's all for her an' the baby. But she can't see that. Thinks I enjoy bein' cooped up in some office 60-plus hours a week... Well she's got another thing comin'!

PAUL. I think you mean *think*.

IAN. Thing, think... Don't go gettin' all grammatical on me! She should be grateful I'm not like my old man. Goddamn deadbeat. Ya know how many times I come home from school, he's cuddled up on the couch with his best friend Colt 45? Meanwhile, my mom's off bustin' her ass at some second job... What guy in his right mind would rather work when he can spend a day at Coney Island with his wife? I keep tellin' her, it's all gonna be worth it. Maybe not right now... But someday.

PAUL. Now ya sound like my partner.

IAN. What's this dude done that's got ya so rattled?

PAUL. Let's just say he hasn't been completely honest.

IAN. So kick 'im to the curb! Life's too short for pussy footin' around.

PAUL. Pussy footin'?

IAN. Don't go gettin' all judge-y on me! Ya need to grow yourself a pair... Give that partner of yours da boot.

PAUL. Sometimes I wish I could.

IAN. Then why don't ya?

PAUL. 'Cause he makes me pancakes for breakfast on Sunday mornin's. An' he never laughs when I cry, an' he cries when he laughs. When we're asleep in bed together, I don't ever wanna wake up. An' when we're awake at night, I don't ever wanna go to sleep. He's the first guy I fell in love with... An' when it comes down to it, I don't care if he ever talks to his parents 'bout me or not. He's the one I wanna marry... Not them.

IAN. So why ya tellin' *me* all-a this?

> *LIGHTS FADE on IAN and PAUL, come UP on MARK and STACY.*

MARK. When does old Brown Eyes return?

STACY. Tomorrow afternoon... Or so he says.

MARK. What are you ladies doing with the rest of your alone-time?

STACY. Hanging out with you.

> *MARK's cell phone RINGS. HE checks the caller-ID display.*

MARK. It's Paul... *(HE answers as a now-sober PAUL appears, Starbucks in hand.)* What's up?

PAUL. Hey, hon.

STACY. Hey, Paul!

MARK. Stacy says hey...

PAUL. Hello.

MARK. We're sitting on the Promenade watching the sunset.

PAUL. No fair... I wanna sit on the Promenade watching the sunset.

> *MARK looks at PAUL. THEY speak directly to each other.*

MARK. I'm glad you called.

PAUL. You are?

MARK. I got some bad news. I talked to my dad earlier...

PAUL. You did?

MARK. My Uncle Gene passed away.

PAUL. I'm sorry.

MARK. The funeral's on Saturday... I'll be coming up to Boston on Friday morning.

MARK. I was thinking maybe we could spend the whole weekend together... Maybe the whole week.

PAUL. I wish I could...

MARK. But you can't?

PAUL. I'm flying to LA on Tuesday morning.

MARK. You hate "La."

PAUL. Don't remind me.

MARK. What's in LA?

PAUL. Bullshit meeting with some client... I'll be back on Thursday night.

MARK. Well try to hurry... I can only take so much drama on *The Bob & Helen Gray Show.*

PAUL. Make sure you pick up your absentee ballot for the primary...

MARK. Tuesday's the 11th already? Shit.

PAUL. Unless you *want* Mike Bloomberg as your next mayor.

MARK. You sure are funny.

PAUL. I'm cute too. *(beat)* You didn't tell your father about us, did you?

MARK. Not yet... But I will.

PAUL. Please don't.

MARK. I thought that's what you wanted.

PAUL. You know what they say: "It's a gay man's prerogative to change his mind."

LIGHTS FADE.

SCENE 4

Thursday. IAN appears on his cell phone.

IAN. Hey, honey. It's me... It's Thursday around 5. Why aren't you answering your cell phone? I'm still in Boston. I missed my flight. There's another one at 5:30, gets in at 6:38. With any luck, I should be home by 7:10 — 7:20 at the latest... Don't leave for birthing class without me, okay?

> *HE hangs up and FADES away as LIGHTS come UP on STACY and MARK in the brownstone.*

STACY. What time is it?

MARK. 7:40.

STACY. All we've done for the past six days is sleep in, go to Starbucks, and sit on the Promenade. The one night we finally have something important to do, Ian can't be bothered. *(beat)* That's it! If this is how it's going to be for the next ten years, I want out.

MARK. And they say I'm the drama queen.

STACY. I'm telling you, I can't take it anymore.

MARK. What exactly were you expecting when you got married? And please don't tell me: a white picket fence.

STACY. I expected my husband to be around when I needed him.

MARK. Well I hate to play Devil's Advocate...

STACY. Then don't.

MARK. You knew what kinda work Ian did when you met him.

STACY. Yes...

MARK. Wasn't he just as busy then as he is now?

STACY. Yes...

MARK. So how has anything changed?

STACY. Because back then... I was busy too.

MARK. Which is why you hit it off.

STACY. I hate you.

MARK. Let's go, princess! I'm taking you to birthing class. Then I'm bringing you back home... When we get here, Ian will be waiting.

STACY. Unless...

MARK. Unless what?

STACY. We don't come home.

MARK. Now why would you wanna do such a crazy thing?

STACY. We can always stay with my parents in Greenwich for a while. Or...

MARK. Don't even think it.

STACY. Maybe we can crash at your place.

MARK. Now why would you wanna do such a crazy thing?

STACY. We'll sleep on the couch.

MARK. For starters, it's a *futon*. And number B... I wouldn't let my worst enemy sleep on that thing. *(beat)* Okay, maybe my worst.

STACY. What about your new best friend?

LIGHTS FADE on STACY and MARK as IAN enters the brownstone, travel bag slung over his shoulder.

IAN. Honey...? *(HE checks the time, exits into the other room.)* Stacy...? *(HE returns, dialing his cell. No answer. HE hangs up, dials again.)* Hey, Sylvia. *(Pause.)* It's your son-in-law... I seem to have misplaced my wife. *(Pause.)* I know, I'm supposed to go with her. *(Pause.)* I did try her cell phone. *(Pause.)* I *would* — if I knew where they're having it at. *(Pause.)* No, no. No worries... I'll find her.

IAN hangs up. HE comes across STACY's sweater, breathes in her scent as LIGHTS FADE, come UP on MARK and STACY in MARK's apartment.

MARK. I was gonna alphabetize my CD collection... But I gotta admit: playing surrogate daddy with a bunch of fat, sweaty, hormonal women was much more exciting.

STACY. Thanks for keeping me company.

MARK. What are neighbors for? Borrowing a cup of sugar... Feeding the cat while you're away... Holding your hand at birthing class when your husband's off with She-Who-Must-Not-Be-Named.

LIGHTS UP on IAN, dialing his cell phone. STACY's cell phone begins to RING. SHE checks the caller-ID, does not answer.

STACY. It's not like I didn't warn him.

IAN. Damn it, Stacy! Where are you?

HE hangs up and FADES away.

MARK. What if he calls the police?

STACY. Ian? Please! The man abandoned his pregnant wife... Who in their right mind would have any sympathy?

MARK. If you don't call him back, I will.

STACY. You don't know his number.

MARK. I can just as easily walk next door.

STACY. You wouldn't dare.

MARK. Wanna test me? Call him.

STACY. No.

MARK. Are you always this stubborn?

STACY. I'm a woman.

MARK. 'Cause the boobs and the bun in the oven kinda threw me.

STACY. Just let us stay here tonight... We need some time to think.

MARK. You and Little Lahna need to go home.

STACY. To what? A husband who doesn't give a shit if we're there or not.

MARK. I could never say no to a bully.

STACY. Thank you.

MARK. It's a lucky thing I did my laundry.

STACY. Just tell us where the clean sheets are...

MARK. Oh no, I'll get 'em... You're the squatter.

STACY. No, no. We insist... Besides, I could stand to partake of the facilities while I'm up.

MARK. You just went!

STACY. Chihuahua bladder, remember?

MARK. That's what you get for making me stop at Starbucks.

STACY. I made you! Who's the junkie now, bub?

> *SHE exits. After a moment, MARK spies STACY's cell phone. HE picks it up, scrolls through the contacts list.*

MARK. *(to himself)* Change Mark Gay to *Gray*... *(HE corrects the mistake, scrolls through again, can't find what he's looking for, scrolls back.)* Under B for Brown Eyes? Oh Stacy...

> *MARK dials. IAN's cell phone begins to RING. HE checks the caller-ID display, answers.*

IAN. Stacy! Where are you? I been sick to my stomach —

MARK. Ian, hey...

IAN. Who the fuck is this?

MARK. My name's Mark... I'm a friend of Stacy's. *(beat)* Bench guy.

IAN. Where's she at?

MARK. She wanted me to call and let you know she's okay.

STACY. *(off)* Mark!

IAN. Tell her I need her.

MARK. You need to tell her yourself.

STACY. *(off)* Mark!

MARK. 128 Willow Street... Buzzer number G.

> *HE hangs up. LIGHTS FADE on IAN as STACY appears.*

STACY. We couldn't find the — *(SHE notices MARK holding her phone.)* Who are you talking to?

MARK. Um... Paul called.

STACY. Why was Paul calling you on *my* cell phone?

> *SOUND of doorbell BUZZ.*

MARK. I'm sorry... But as a good neighbor, I can't consciously allow you to hide out from your husband in my apartment.

> *HE gives STACY her cell, buzzes IAN in.*

STACY. So much for my new best friend.

> *A KNOCK on the door. MARK opens it as IAN bursts into the room.*

IAN. Stacy!

MARK. You must be Ian... I'm Mark Gray.

STACY. Stage name, Benedict Arnold.

IAN. Hey, honey.

STACY. I'm mad at you.

MARK. And I'm walking away.

> *HE exits.*

IAN. Hey there, Little Lahna.

STACY. Lahna's not speaking to you either.

IAN. Then would you please tell her: Daddy misses her and wishes she would come home?

STACY. Daddy should've thought of that before he skipped her first birthing class.

IAN. My cab got stuck in traffic. I tried calling but I kept getting your voice mail... I'm sorry you had to go all by yourself.

STACY. Don't be sorry... Mark took us.

IAN. Who is this Mark guy anyways?

STACY. He's a friend.

IAN. Well you can't stay here tonight.

STACY. Why not? You stayed overnight in Boston with Miss Tits.

IAN. You think I'm sleeping with Rachel?

STACY. Would you even tell me if you were?

IAN. I'm not!

STACY. Why should I believe you?

IAN. 'Cause I said so.

STACY. It's not enough anymore.

> *SHE shows IAN the door.*

IAN. "If that's what Mrs. Brown wants..."

> *HE exits. After a moment, MARK appears.*

MARK. Is everything okay?

STACY. Everything is most definitely not okay.

> *LIGHTS FADE.*

SCENE 5

MARK and PAUL alone together.

MARK. Take me away from this place.

PAUL. Where would you like to go?

MARK. How about Maui?

PAUL. I love Maui!

MARK. I know you do.

PAUL. What'll we do with ourselves?

MARK. Open up a shave-ice truck and eat banana-macadamia nut pancakes.

PAUL. And lie in the sun all day and grow old together.

MARK. Till death do us part.

PAUL. What about your parents?

MARK. I told them.

PAUL. Get the fuck out! At your uncle's funeral?

MARK. You should've been there.

PAUL. I'm sorry I missed it.

MARK. My mother cried.

PAUL. What did your father say?

MARK. You were right.

PAUL. I'm proud of you.

MARK. The whole thing was pretty simple, really... We were standing around chit-chatting. What a great guy Uncle Gene was. Blah blah blah... To which my mother chimes in: "Too bad he wasted his life." To which I reply: "Guess what, Ma? I'm wastin' my life too."

PAUL. What made you change your mind?

MARK. Knowing I might lose you forever if I didn't.

> *STACY appears in MARK's apartment.*

STACY. Happy Friday!

> *MARK looks to STACY then back at PAUL.*

MARK. "I am afeard/Being in night, all this is but a dream/Too flattering-sweet to be substantial."

> *LIGHTS CHANGE. It was indeed only a daydream and PAUL FADES away, leaving MARK and STACY alone together.*

STACY. Is everything all right?

MARK. Everything is most definitely not all right.

STACY. I'm heading up to Greenwich to see my parents for the weekend... Maybe longer.

MARK. You are not leaving Ian.

STACY. I don't know what I'm doing anymore.

MARK. Have you talked to him this morning?

STACY. He left yet another message.

MARK. And...?

STACY. He wants to meet for lunch in the city.

MARK. So go.

STACY. He'll never change.

MARK. Maybe you need to accept that.

STACY. Why should I be the one to give in?

MARK. 'Cause we do that sometimes... When we love somebody.

STACY. Maybe it's time *you* give in.

MARK. And do what?

STACY. It's not like you'd be the first gay man ever to disappoint his parents... So they get pissed off? It's the 21st century, they'll get over it. And if they don't, as my *bubbe* used to say: "No big whoop!" You've still got Paul. *(beat)* Though to be honest, I don't see why he's put up with you for this long.

MARK. Ouch.

STACY. The truth's a bitch, ain't it?

MARK. I'm beginning to think I could say the same thing about you.

STACY. I'm only trying to help.

MARK. Paul's the one who changed his mind... I was all set to talk to my folks this weekend.

STACY. Please! Do you really think that's what Paul wants? But he loves you, so he gave you an out.

MARK. You obviously have no idea what I'm going through.

STACY. You don't think my parents had a total conniption when I married a *goy* from New Jersey? And a *schvartze* at that! The first time I mentioned the name Ian Brown, they practically disowned me.

MARK. This isn't some trust fund we're talking about losing here —

STACY. Tell that to Murray and Sylvia Gold.

MARK. My parents could cut me out of their lives forever and then what would I do?

STACY. From everything you've told me, you'd be better off.

MARK. No offense, Stacy... But you've never met my parents, okay? Everything I've done by not telling them about me, I've done out of a place of love. *For them.* They don't understand the first thing about what it means to be gay... And neither do their church going, pinochle playing, moonlight bowling friends. So if I can spare them some of the pain and rejection I've had to deal with, what's a little secret gonna hurt?

STACY. Fine... Protect your parents from the cold, cruel world. Choose their love over a man who wants to spend the rest of his life with you. What do I care if *you* don't?

MARK. Who are you to lecture me? Ian's busting his ass to give you and Lahna everything you could possibly ever need... And all you've done since day one is whine about it.

STACY. Oh my god... That is so not true.

MARK. Oh my god... It totally is! Ian doesn't want you to work. Ian's never around. Ian's off somewhere fucking Rachel... So what if he is? You wouldn't be the first wife ever to have a cheating husband.

STACY. Wow! "With friends like you..."

MARK. Then maybe we shouldn't be.

STACY. If that's how you feel...

    SHE gathers her things.

MARK. *(an apology)* Stacy...

STACY. I feel sorry for you, Mark. No... I take that back. I feel sorry for Paul. He seems like a really great guy.

*SHE exits. MARK stands in silence a moment
then finds his cell phone and dials.*

MARK. *(Southie accent)* Hey, Pop. It's ya son... There's somethin' we gotta talk about when I'm home this weekend.

LIGHTS FADE.

SCENE 6

IAN and STACY alone together.

IAN. Happy Anniversary!

HE produces a Starbucks coffee.

STACY. *Who* are you and *what* have you done with my husband?

IAN. Iced decaf venti, sugar-free vanilla, nonfat, no whip, mocha.

STACY. You remembered.

IAN. What kinda man forgets his wife's favorite drink from Starbucks?

STACY. I'm not talking about the Starbucks.

IAN. Somebody isn't ready.

STACY. Are we going somewhere?

IAN. I took a whole day off to do something special with my girls... By gum, I'm doing it!

STACY. By gum?

IAN. Lahna... Tell Mommy not to make fun of Daddy.

STACY. Tell Daddy not to act like such a *schmuck*!

IAN. Tell Mommy she's the one who married a *schmuck*.

STACY. It's a lucky thing you're cute.

IAN. I'm funny too.

SOUND of CONEY ISLAND as LIGHTS CHANGE.

STACY. Ian! Is it really — ?

IAN. Welcome to Coney Island! And to your left, ladies and germs... Nathan's Famous hot dogs.

STACY. I bet they're not as tasty as the free ones at Rudy's.

IAN. What's say we try a couple and find out?

STACY. "If that's what Mr. Brown wants..."

> *SHE quickly disappears.*

IAN. Stacy, wait!

> *SOUND of THUNDER. IAN looks around
> in a panic.*

IAN. Stacy...? *(No response.)* Stacy...?!

> *LIGHTS CHANGE. It was only a daydream.
> IAN is now safe inside the brownstone as
> RAIN begins to fall.*

IAN. So much for Coney Island. *(HE takes out his cell, dials.)* Hey, Howard. Ian Brown. The meeting's all set for tomorrow morning. 8:30 in the conference room... Listen, something's come up. I can't make it. It's mine and Stacy's anniversary —

> *STACY appears in the brownstone, brandishing
> a soggy umbrella.*

STACY. Ian...?

IAN. Honey, you're home!

> *HE hangs up.*

STACY. So are you... In the middle of a Monday afternoon.

IAN. I got a meeting with a client in The Slope... I dropped by to pick up some papers. *(beat)* How was Greenwich?

STACY. Chilly... I forgot my sweater.

IAN. It's nice and warm here in Brooklyn Heights.

STACY. It's raining.

IAN. A little rain never hurt nobody.

STACY. This is more than just a little rain.

> *LIGHTS FADE on IAN and STACY, come UP on MARK and PAUL in Boston.*

MARK. Surprise!

> *HE produces a small box.*

PAUL. What's this?

MARK. Looks like a little box.

PAUL. What's in it?

MARK. Maybe you should open it and find out.

> *LIGHTS UP on IAN and STACY.*

IAN. I took the day off tomorrow...

> *PAUL opens the box to reveal a silver ring.*

> PAUL. Nice... What's it for?

STACY. Whatever for?

> *MARK drops to one knee.*

> MARK. Will you marry me?

IAN. Come with me to Coney Island?

PAUL. Can we have a big party and register for gifts?

STACY. Can we ride the Wonder Wheel and get stuck at the tippy-top?

MARK. If that's what my lover wants...

IAN. "If that's what Mrs. Brown wants..."

PAUL. I do.

HE kisses MARK.

STACY. I do.

SHE kisses IAN.

MARK. I can't wait to pledge my love for you in front of everybody... Including my parents.

IAN's cell RINGs.

IAN. I'm not answering it.

PAUL. I'm not going to LA.

STACY. You have to...

MARK. You'll be back...

IAN. Not right now.

PAUL. Not for two whole days.

126

*STACY holds her
belly.*

STACY. We can wait.

                MARK. We waited this long...

IAN. Lemme get rid of
him, okay?

                PAUL. Let me give you my
                flight info...

*IAN answers his cell phone as PAUL searches for
his itinerary.*

IAN. Hey, Howard... *(Pause.)* Yeah I left you a message...
(Pause.) No shit! Kyle's first day of kindergarten already?
You're his old man... You gotta take him. *(Pause.).* I won't
be at the meeting... I'm taking Stacy to Coney Island.

                MARK. Paul?

STACY. Ian?

                PAUL. Be right there!

IAN. I can't be there.

                MARK. Paul?

STACY. Ian?

                PAUL. One second!

                HE locates the itinerary.

IAN. *(to STACY)* Honey,
one sec.

                PAUL. Here we go, hon...

STACY. Tell Howard you'll
come to the meeting.

MARK. *(reading)* 7:45 AM... American Airlines... Flight number 11.

IAN. But tomorrow's our anniversary.

PAUL. Flight 11 on September 11?

STACY. It's just another day.

BLACK OUT.

EPILOGUE

LIGHTS UP on IAN and PAUL both dressed for another day. THEY speak to the audience as STACY and MARK wait nearby.

IAN. Tuesday morning...

PAUL. We lie in bed...

IAN. I stand by the bed...

PAUL. Breathing as one...

IAN. Watching her sleep...

PAUL. So peaceful.

IAN. So beautiful.

PAUL. Have a great day!

IAN. I love you.

PAUL. I love you.

IAN. Have a great day!

PAUL. Why does our time together never seem long enough?

IAN. Why does the call of duty always carry me away?

PAUL. It's just another day...

IAN. Like so many before it.

PAUL. Like so many before it...

IAN. It's just another day.

PAUL. Another day of airports...

IAN. Another day of office buildings.

PAUL. Of lovers living their lives apart...

IAN. Separated by distances long and short.

PAUL. It's just another day in the city of Boston...

IAN. Here in New York City, it's just another day...

PAUL. And yet —

>*HE stops himself.*

IAN. And yet —

>*HE stops himself.*

PAUL. Outside the weather is perfect...

IAN. A perfect day outside...

PAUL. Not a cloud in the sky...

IAN. The sky so blue...

PAUL. It's the most beautiful day I've ever seen.

IAN. The most beautiful day.

PAUL. Once I arrive, I pass through security...

IAN. After I arrive, I step through security...

PAUL. Make my way over to gate B-32.

IAN. Take the elevators up to the 105th floor.

PAUL. I board the plane...

IAN. I enter my office...

PAUL. Sit down in my seat...

IAN. Sit down at my desk...

PAUL. Around 8:15... It begins.

IAN. Around 8:45... It begins.

PAUL. I look out the window...

IAN. I look out my window...

PAUL. I see blue skies...

IAN. The city there before me...

PAUL. I see buildings...

IAN. The blue Tuesday all around me...

>*PAUL looks at MARK.*

PAUL. I see Mark.

>*IAN looks at STACY.*

IAN. I see Stacy.

>*SOUND of THUNDER followed by the deafening ROAR of the World as it comes crashing down.*

>*After a moment, all is SILENT. Then...*

>*MUSIC: Billie Holiday's "Without Your Love."*

>*BOTH COUPLES come together and dance.*

>*After a mutual kiss goodbye, IAN and PAUL FADE away, leaving STACY and MARK alone together.*

>*MARK places his hand on STACY's stomach. SHE lets out a gasp as the baby kicks.*

>*LIGHTS FADE.*

END OF PLAY

ABOUT THE AUTHOR

FRANK ANTHONY POLITO is the Publisher of Woodward Avenue Books, named for the famed "M-1" thoroughfare linking the Motor City to its suburbs.

He received his BFA in Theatre from Wayne State and his MFA in Dramatic Writing from Carnegie Mellon. Other plays include *Band Fags!*, based on his award-winning novel, and *Blue Tuesday*, the one-act precursor to *Another Day on Willow St.*

Published books include *Band Fags!* (InsightOut Book Club – Best Fiction), *Drama Queers!* (Lambda Literary Award), *Remembering Christmas* (featuring the sequel to *Band Fags!*, "A Christmas to Remember"), *Lost in the '90s*, and *The Spirit of Detroit*, the third novel in the "Hazeltucky" trilogy.

Frank grew up in the Detroit suburb of Hazel Park. He currently resides in Pleasant Ridge, MI with his partner, Craig Bentley, for whom he wrote the role of "Mark" in *Another Day on Willow St*, and their beagle mix puppy Clyde.

For more info visit: www.frankanthonypolito.com

www.ingramcontent.com/pod-product-compliance
Lightning Source LLC
Chambersburg PA
CBHW050947030426
42339CB00007B/324